STEPPES
TO
NEU ODESSA

Germans from Russia
Who Settled in
Odessa Township,
Dakota Territory
1872-1876

- Second Edition -

Cynthia Anne Frank Stupnik

HERITAGE BOOKS
2009

HERITAGE BOOKS
AN IMPRINT OF HERITAGE BOOKS, INC.

Books, CDs, and more—Worldwide

For our listing of thousands of titles see our website
at
www.HeritageBooks.com

Published 2009 by
HERITAGE BOOKS, INC.
Publishing Division
100 Railroad Ave. #104
Westminster, Maryland 21157

International Standard Book Numbers
Paperbound: 978-0-7884-2120-4
Clothbound: 978-0-7884-8102-4

Here's what others are saying about

Steppes to Neu-Odessa

Stupnik's book vividly portrays the development of this area of South Dakota by German from Russia families who were homesteaders in the 1870's. Her excellent research on specific families shown on the homestead maps gives an interesting account of these families and their descendants. This book is very valuable for those who can trace their roots back to this community.

—Delmar Hofer, Ed. D.,
Retired Educator, Elderhostel Coordinator, Hutterite Centennial Committee

These are our ancestors, the first four groups of German Russians from the Black Sea area who found in 1872 near Yankton similarly rich wheat soil to the Russian steppes they had left. Between the genealogical facts of their lives - birth, death and marriage dates - emerge glimpses of the community they built. Dugouts and sod houses grow into botza brick and wooden frame dwellings, with stables nearly as big as their houses. Original documents, among them homestead applications, land patent records, and photos, add richness to the documentation of our past while newspaper clippings give us a taste of everyday life. An adventurous 4-year-old falls 22 feet of the roof of his family's store, walking away with only a few bruises. A mother of six dies in childbirth. A resident returns to Russia for a visit, but would never live there again, even "if they would give me the best farm in the country." I'm honored that my work supplied a few puzzle pieces to this most helpful and satisfying research tool.

—Sally Roesch Wagner, Ph.D.
Author, *Daughter of Dakota* series

One can follow the circuitous emigrations of the first Germans from Russia to settle in Dakota Territory - from Germany and Poland to South Russia, Sandusky, Ohio, Dakota Territory, and points north and west - through the newspaper articles and family records, which provide interesting and enjoyable reading.

—Janice Huber Stangl
Co-Author of *Marienberg - Fate of a Village*

This book is dedicated to my father

Harold F. Frank
1912-1994

because even though he was an orphan,
he instilled in me pride for my
German Russian heritage.

C. M. & St. P. Depot, Yankton, S. D.

Depot in Yankton, Dakota Territory, where many German Russians arrived.

Table of Contents

Illustrations

Documents

xi

Acknowledgments

A thank you to all of those who gave me permission to quote from their books: Walter Kusler, *The Kuslers and Their Descendants*; Armand Bauer and Dr. LaVern Rippley, *Russia-German Settlements in the United States*; Curtis Media Corporation and the Yankton County Historical Society, *History of Yankton County*; Sally Roesch Wagner, *Daughters of Dakota: Schooled in Privation*; County Atlas Company, *Odessa Township Homestead Map of Yankton County*; Glen Gering and the Pine Hill Press, Inc., *MENNO: The First 100 Years 1879-1979*; Dr. Hans Rath and Betty Rath, *The Black Sea Germans in the Dakotas*; Germans from Russia Heritage Society, various issues of the *Heritage Review* and publishing "'The Rooshuns'" in 1995; American Historical Society of Germans from Russia, *The Emigration from Germany to Russia in the Years 1763 to 1862* and *Work Paper No. 12*.

Thank you to the following who provided information in letter form: Julian Keithahn for Berndts, Serrs, Jasmanns, Engels and a photograph of the Serrs; Deborah Rothery for the families of Kosts and Kuslers; Norman Schamber for Schamber information; Curt Renz for Engels, Berndts and Boettchers; Eugene Weidenbach for the Weidenbach family information; and Della Kiesz for Engels and Serrs and photographs of Serrs and Stollers.

A special thank you to Amelia Weidenbach for all of her time and interest in the research of not only her information on the members of the Weidenbach family, but for information on almost everyone else in Odessa Township. Another thanks to my sister Rebecca Frank for her help in combing through county courthouses and her insight into my ability to accomplish this task.

I also want to thank the Odessa group, Dale Wahl, Roger Ehrich, Marty McMahon, and countless others who have provided the Digital Library of resources, including the St. Petersburg Archives, cemetery lists, village compilations, and census and ship records that have helped me continue my research for ancestors and individuals settling in Odessa Township, Yankton County.

Preface

Odessa Township, Yankton County, Dakota Territory, received its name from the many Germans who came from Russia between 1872-1876. Many individuals, who are equally important in the German-Russian settlement in Dakota Territory, are not listed in this biographical dictionary because they happened to homestead across county and township lines. Individuals like Dominik Stoller, Conrad and Jacob Weidenbach, Peter Moos, Gottfried Mehrer, Jacob Weber, Balthasar and Johann Hauck, Jacob Gimble, and Peter, Anton, and Philip Orth helped others gain the courage to homestead in a foreign land.

ODESSA HOMESTEAD TOWNSHIP MAP

TOWNSHIP: 96N
RANGE: 57W.

JAMES RIVER

Map of original homesteads in Odessa Township. Used with permission of
County Atlas Company.

Odessa Township

Township 96N Range 57W

6	5	4	3	2	1
7	8		10	11	12
18	17	16 E	15	14	13
19	20	21	22	23	24
30	29	28 C	27	26	25
B 31	32	33	D 34	35	36

A

James River

South Dakota Highway 46

A. St. Petersburg German Congregational Cemetery
southwest corner of southwest quarter of section 31

B. German Reformed Odessa Cemetery
southwest quarter of northeast quarter of section 31

C. Evangelical Lutheran Zions Gemeinde of Yankton County (cemetery)
southwest quarter of section 28

D. Hoffnung Reformed Cemetery
southeast corner of northeast quarter of section 34

E. Horst Private Cemetery
northwest corner of northwest quarter of section 15

INTRODUCTION

W hen Catherine II (1762-1796) wanted to upgrade the Russian agricultural system, she issued a manifesto to western European countries calling for hard working people to settle near St. Petersburg and areas near the Volga shore. Along with inhabitants from other countries, thousands of German citizens answered the call. Later, on February 20, 1804, her grandson, Alexander I, also invited heads of households of selected families to move into the Black Sea area. He asserted that these people would be models for the Russians and Ukrainians in terms of agriculture and trade. The manifesto required that any person entering Russia to settle also had to "present certificates" written by the authorities from his country to the Russian authorities stating that he was diligent and respectful. In return for the immigrants' exemplary lifestyles, the Russian government promised the colonists many important things, but the most important were freedom of religion, freedom from taxes, and freedom from military service.[1] Again, Germans accepted the invitation. By 1859 the German population had reached 143,733.[2] But for many of these German colonists who worked so hard to own their own land and maintain their own culture, this would not be their final stop.

For a period, the Russian government appreciated the German colonists for the way they made the steppes as well as their own lives so productive. As farmers, they did not live on separate, isolated farms, but in neatly arranged villages called dorfs. From their houses, often white-stuccoed dwellings with house and barn under one roof, the farmers went out every day to tend to their livestock, but their fields were farther out on the steppes.[3] The Germans built up the 30 to 60 hectares of land that Russian authorities allotted them and then purchased more. They raised many types of grains, but they were especially successful in growing wheat. In the districts closer to the Black Sea, as well as the Crimea, Bessarabia, and the Transcaucasus region, they also had substantial vineyards. In the field of animal husbandry, the German farmers raised sheep, but they also developed and became renowned for special breeds of cows and horses called "German Red Cows" and "German Horses" that were especially suited for Russia's harsh climate.[4]

As the emperors requested, the Germans were excellent role models for the Russians and Ukrainians because they were hard working, industrious, and extremely religious. Because of the German colonists' dedication to hard work, the Ukraine became known as "the bread basket of Europe."[5] They were also industrious in the field of education. The German schools, while still not as advanced as in their motherland, were still way ahead of Russian schools. According to an 1897 Russian census, "78% of the Russian citizenry was still illiterate while the overwhelming majority of the Germans in the Russian villages could read and write." [6] The colonists' zest for religion was as strong as their zest for work. While most of the Black Sea Germans were of the Lutheran confession, there were also many who belonged to the Evangelical, Catholic, Mennonite, and Separatist religious organizations. Each village, with a rare exception, was centered around the Germans' religious affiliation, with the church and prayer halls in the heart of the village. Although the Germans were proud of their nationality, they seldom intermingled with other Germans outside of their professed faith.[7]

For as much as the Germans were respected by the Ukrainians and Russians because of their hardworking, moral lifestyles, they were eventually looked upon with jealousy and rivalry by the native population. The Russian people were not happy with their own conditions. For centuries the Russian population had been under a yoke of servility working for feudal lords. In fact, they had to pay taxes on the little bit of land they called their own. In addition, the males had to serve for a period in the Russian military, protecting its borders from the almost constant threat of attack by foreigners. Russian citizens also had to follow the doctrines of the Greek Orthodox Church.

On the other hand, according to all of the agreements that brought them into a foreign land, many of the Russians believed that the Germans were treated as though they were honored guests in a land that they did not have to help support. They paid no taxes on the amassed sums they made on the land that the government had freely given them. The German males did not serve in the Russian military. And, according to the mandate their fathers and forefathers had agreed upon, they could worship when, where, and whatever religion they wanted. But even though the Russians knew that the Germans, along with the other foreigners, had been invited into their country under special conditions, a Nationalistic movement formed within the native population, especially the "upper classes." The individuals instrumental in the movement believed that all of the "nationalities were strangers, were foreign, Catholic or Protestant, in no way Russian.… German colonists were the objects of hatred for the upper classes who did not want to admit that this group had helped to build up the country. They despised these colonists especially because they refused to become Russian in religion and culture."[8]

In part, the schools and churches were responsible for this because they taught, preached, read, and spoke German, which kept the colonists "self-sufficient and independent."[9] Even though the Germans had always been friendly in their associations with the native neighbors, they had never been made to assimilate. In fact, they "felt culturally, socially, and even racially superior to their Russian or Tartar neighbors throughout their stay with them."[10] Because of this, the Germans not only took seriously the promises made by previous rulers, but they also became stubbornly committed to maintaining their own culture and nationality.

After nearly 100 years, the Russian society's complaints against the Germans finally got through to the emperor. In 1871, Russianization began. The "taking away of privileges…was only the beginning."[11] Additionally, it was announced that the male colonists had to start serving in the military. Finally, "[t]hey had to become Greek Orthodox and Russian."[12]

The Germans became agitated and concerned with the new prescripts forced upon them by the Russian government. They started looking for other lands in which to live. While some

xix

colonists considered Palestine and Argentina as possibilities, other German Russian colonists directed their attention to America.

The first four groups of German Russians from the Black Sea area arrived in the United States in 1872. That first winter, they stayed in Sandusky, Ohio, with relatives who had migrated much earlier. In the spring of 1873, the immigrants "'agreed to send out scouts (Kindschafter) to look around for land that would suit them as a group.'"[13] The scouts went south and west, through Michigan, Iowa, Nebraska, Minnesota, Kansas, Missouri, and Arkansas, but they did not find what they wanted. Frederick Mutschelknaus, an early settler, reported,

> 'Finally, they were told to go to Dakota, to the city of Yankton; there they probably would find it the way they wanted...farther to the north there were still government lands which could be gotten as homesteads. After looking it over, the delegation liked the land so well that it decided to recommend Dakota for settlement....They told the people that they had seen green wheat and that the farmers at Yankton had told them that they had sown the seed at the end of February. It was almost like in Russia.[14]

The scouts found that the land to be homesteaded north of Yankton, Dakota Territory, was similar to the rich black soil they had been farming near Odessa on the coast of the Black Sea. After they sent letters back home to family and friends in Russia, the first influx of German Russians arrived in America. In George Kingsbury's *History of Dakota Territory*, the number of Germans entering the United States from Russia was "about one hundred thousand during the decade beginning in 1871, and of this number many thousands found homes on the virgin prairies of Dakota Territory." The first groups to arrive settled about twenty miles northwest of Yankton, Dakota Territory. Homesteaders gave the first settlement the name of "Odessa" in remembrance of the great port on the Black Sea.[15]

The Yankton Press, Yankton County, Dakota Territory, 4 April 1873:

A LARGE RUSSIAN COLONY TO SETTLE IN DAKOTA

Four gentlemen, representing a large colony of German Russians, had an audience yesterday with Gen. McCook, Judge Brookings, Hon. G.H. Hand, Postmaster McIntyre and others, at Gen. McCook's office. Simon Eiseman acted as interpreter. At the close of the interview they expressed themselves well pleased with information derived in regard to the country. They have made arrangements to start today for the upper Dakota river to select a location. We understand the colony consists of from one hundred to one thousand families. One hundred families will locate during the early spring, and the remainder of one thousand will settle as soon as they can cross the ocean.

The Yankton Press 14 May 1873:

THE GERMAN-RUSSIANS

...we now understand they have stuck their stakes in the northern portion of Yankton County. Three townships of land have already been selected contiguous to the "noble Jim," and on these fertile acres will the present advance guard locate. Surveyors are now at work laying off the claims, and the colonists have already begun work.

The Yankton Press 20 August 1873:

Our German immigrants are making times lively in this section. $1000 bills are in circulation, and about 50 farm houses are under contract and are being framed by Yankton mechanics for these people. Our lumber merchants, hardware men, dry goods dealers and live stock [*sic*] owners are reaping a greenback harvest—in fact everybody is making more money than they ever did before. Verily, the good time has come.

The Yankton Press 27 August 1873:

THE RUSSIANS

I find here a large number of the much talked of natives of Russland. They do not claim to belong to the same class or sect that have thought of settling in Minnesota, though of German origin. Instead of being Mennonites, they are mainly Lutherans, with Quakerish views in regard to bearing arms. By a late edict of the Russian Czar they will be compelled to not only bear arms as other subjects, but also to support the Greek or national church. From an interview with some of the leaders, of Yankton, I have learned many things connected with their history and manners of living. They are nearly all farmers of means, their principal business having been that of wheat culture near Odessa on the Black Sea. The country north of this place suits them and some seventy-five families are on the ground or to arrive in a few days. Many more are to come on hereafter. The absence of timber does not frighten those farmers, as they intend to use straw for fuel as in the old country.

L. M. Ford

The "Rooshuns"

In quest of home, they roamed Dakota's range.
From Yankton to Pembina, wagon wheels
dug furrows these tenacious nomads trekked
to claim near-similes of Ukraine's steppes.

They settled. Waist-high grasses waved and clapped
an encore: soddies, shanties, rammed-earth shacks
cropped up. The husbandmen corralled the land
like bronco busters broke the untamed west.

Grooms planted rows of barley, wheat, and corn.
Their wives nursed fragile sprigs of cottownwoods.
Stacks of *mischt*, the twists of tight-wound hay
became crude symbols of their brutal lives.

These pacifists fought wars against the snows,
against the droughts and fires, the storms of ice.
Once former subjects, nouveau czars of plains,
in black knee boots, stood firm on humble realms.

I see them in gray photos: faces grave,
babushkas, sheepskin coats, beside their squats.
I read church records, letters, homestead deeds,
a diary, our Bible's family tree.

On page, I transcribe lowly family myths,
then fantasize I enter their domains.
Like Russian thistles, tangled in my thoughts,
dwell pioneers whose blood thins in my veins.

Cynthia Stupnik
1993*

* First published by the Germans from Russia Heritage Society in *Heritage Review*,
Vol. 23, No. 2, June 1993.

[1] Rath, George, *The Black Sea Germans in the Dakotas.* Freeman, South Dakota: Pine Hill Press, 1977, pp. 1, 2.

[2] *Heritage Review*, Bismarck, North Dakota: North Dakota Historical Society of Germans from Russia, June 1973, p. 22.

[3] Sallet, Richard, *Russian-German Settlements in the United States.* Fargo, North Dakota: North Dakota Institute for Regional Studies, 1974, p. 13.

[4] Rath, 23.

[5] Ibid.

[6] Sallet, 14.

[7] Ibid., 12-13.

[8] Rath, 52-53.

[9] Sallet, 14.

[10] Ibid.

[11] Rath, 53.

[12] Ibid., 52.

[13] Ibid., 68.

[14] Ibid., 69.

[15] Ibid., 89.

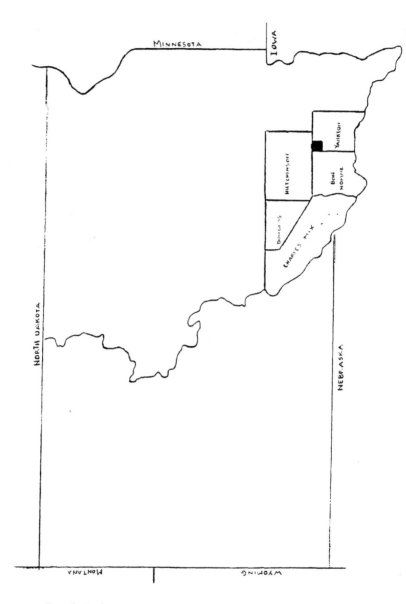

South Dakota map with Odessa Township darkened.
Map by Todd Stupnik.

xxvi

THE SETTLERS

Auch
Heinrich Auch

Heinrich Auch, born 8 May 1861 in Johannestal, South Russia, was the oldest son of **Jacob** and **Rosina Schaefer Auch**.[1] He, along with his parents, arrived in America in 1872 and wintered in Sandusky, Ohio. The Auch family then moved to Dakota Territory in the spring of 1873.

On 16 May 1883, Heinrich applied for naturalization. He homesteaded on the southeast quarter of section 17.

According to the Odessa Reformed Church records, Heinrich Auch married **Elisabetha Weber** 10 November 1885. According to the 1900 U.S. Federal Census for Yankton County and the Odessa Reformed Church records, Elisabeth was born 24 July 1866 and came to America in 1874.

The Auch children were as follows:

1. Emma b 31 October 1886
2. Wilhelm b 7 February 1888
3. Sarah b 28 February 1889
4. Henry b 27 June 1890
5. Lidia b 30 October 1891
6. Lidia Margareth b 1 September 1896
7. Theodor b 20 June 1899
8. John b 19 July 19__
9. Rosina b 21 February 1903
10. Emil b 21 February 190_
11. Ida Christina b 7 February 1907

---

[1] Odessa Digital Library, St. Petersburg Archives, Rohrbach Birth Records, 186x (D. Wahl). http://pixel.cs.vt.edu/library/stpete/rohr/link/rohr186b.txt

Jacob Auch

In 1872 **Jacob** and **Rosina Schafer Auch** were among the first German Russians to leave Johannestal, South Russia, and come to America.[1]

After their voyage on the ship *Leopard*, the family traveled to Sandusky, Ohio, to stay the winter. In spring of 1873, after the scouts found land in Dakota Territory, they settled on the northeast quarters of sections 20 and 21. According to South Dakota naturalization records, Jacob Auch received his final naturalization papers in 1880.

The 1880 U.S. Federal Census states that Jacob was born in Russia, and both of his parents were born in Württemberg, Germany. The St. Petersburg Archives for the "Rohrbach Birth Records, 183x" in the Odessa Digital Library show that Jacob was born on 21 February 1838 in Johannestal to **(Georg) Adam Auch** and **Barbara Schatz**. *(Note: the "x" in the Digital Library citations designates a decade. Thus, "183x" indicates the years 1830-1839; 183b are births from that decade, 183m are marriages, and so on.)* The "Rohrbach Marriage Records, 183x" state that (Georg) Adam's parents were **Gallus** and **Catharina Siegel Auch**. Barbara Schatz Auch's parents were **Jacob** and **Christina Herzel Schatz**. (Georg) Adam Auch and Barbara Schatz were married 31 January 1833 in Rohrbach, South Russia. The church records state that both Georg Adam and Barbara were twenty years old at the time of marriage and from Johannesthal, South Russia.

The *Johannestal, Beresan District Odessa, 1858 Census* indicates that the Auchs arrived in the village in 1816 and lists the children of Georg Adam and Barbara:

1. Barbara, 25, m Stephan Staiger, 25
2. Katharina 23, m Johann Delzer, 25
3. Jakob, 20
4. Elisabetha, 18
5. Christian, 13
6. Friedrich, 10

---

[1] *MENNO: The First 100 Years, 1879-1979*. p. 401 (hereafter referred to as *MENNO*).

Rosina Schafer was born 28 December 1840 in Johannestal, South Russia.[1] The 1880 U.S. Federal Census states that her parents were **Valentin Schaefer** and **Anna Maria Schatz** (see Valentin Schaefer). The Schaefers homesteaded on section 31 in Odessa Township in Yankton County.

According to the German Reformed Odessa Church records, Jacob and Rosina Auch married 26 February 1859 in Johannestal. Jacob Auch was one of the founders of the church, which was located on the northeast quarter of section 31. The same records state the following about the Auch children:

1. Heinrich b 8 May 1861
2. Christian b 29 June 1863*
3. Adam b 17 November 1865*
4. Rosina b 3 February 1868
5. Jacob 4 March 1870
6. Sophia b 18 May 1872
7. Johan b 25 April 1882
8. Agatha b 22 January 1886

Indicates that even though he did not specifically homestead in Odessa Township, I have included his biography following his father's.

After Jacob Auch died, Rosina married **Jacob Kusler** who had homesteaded on the northern half of section 31. By the time of their marriage, Kusler was a storeowner in Scotland, S.D. When he died, Rosina went to live with her daughter **Sophia Auch Horst Winter** near Elgin, North Dakota. (Sophia's first marriage was to the son of **Johann Horst** from section 15.)

The township and range map for 1910 shows that son Johan Auch owned the northeast quarter of section 20 and son Christian owned the northeast quarter of section 21. Rosina Auch owned 120 acres of the southeast quarter of section 17.

Adam Auch, third child of **Jacob** and **Rosina Schaefer Auch**, was born 17 November 1865 in Johannestal, South Russia. He was

---

[1] Odessa Digital Library, St. Petersburg Archives, Rohrbach Birth Records, 184x (D. Wahl). http://pixel.cs.vt.edu/library/stpete/rohr/link/rohr184b.txt

six when he came to America with his parents Jacob and Rosina. *MENNO: The First 100 Years* states this about Auch:

> *The winter of 1871-1872 they spent in Sandusky, Ohio, then he came to Yankton in the spring. On May 3rd, 1872, they moved to their homestead eight miles south of Menno. In 1882, he was apprenticed to a tinsmith. On December 21, 1890, he came to Menno where he practiced his trade as his health would permit.*

Adam married **Elizabeth Knodel** 19 December 1893.[1] The children from that marriage were as follows:

1. Ammon
2. Leiona m Oscar Grossheusch
3. Elma m Richard Weber
4. Martha m Paul Thranum
5. Richard[2]

Christian Auch, second child of Jacob and Rosina Auch, was born 29 June 1863 in Johannstal, South Russia.[3] According to the Odessa Reformed Church records, Christian married **Christina Weber** on 4 December 1888 or 12 April 1888. Christina was born 26 July 1869. They joined the Odessa Reformed Church in 1889.

Their children were as follows:

1. Robert b 31 August 1889
2. Martha b 9 April 1890 or 4 September 1890
3. Sara b 31 January 1894
4. Ferdinant b 6 May 1895
5. Agatha b 1897
6. Leona b 21 October 1898

[1] *MENNO*, p. 401.
[2] *Ibid.*
[3] Odessa Digital Library, St. Petersburg Archives, Rohrbach Birth Records, 186x (D. Wahl). http://pixel.cs.vt.edu/library/stpete/rohr/link/rohr186b.txt

The township and range map for 1910 shows that Christian Auch owned 120 acres of the southern half of section 16 and the northeast quarter of section 21.

Blessing
Johann Blessing
Johann Blessing homesteaded on the northeast quarter of section 35. Although he is not included in the 1880 U.S. Federal Census for Yankton County, he is mentioned in George Kingsbury's *History of Dakota Territory* in the chapter entitled, "The First To Come." He is also listed in the Yankton Naturalization Records as being born in 1857 and arriving in New York in 1874.

Johann was the son of **Wilhelm** and **Christina Maas Blessing**. The "Rohrbach Birth Records, 185x" show that Johann was born 23 June 1857 in Johannesthal. The *Johannestal, Beresan District Odessa, 1858 Census* states that Wilhelm Blessing was the step-son of **Zacharias Ulmer** who was 66 and **Jakobina** who was 59. The records also indicate the Ulmer family arrived in Johannestal in 1831. Wilhelm Blessing's wife Christina was 30. They had the following children at the time: Christoph 6, Louisa 4, Wilhelm 3, Johann 1.

Wilhelm Blessing homesteaded in Yankton County on the southeast quarter of section 11 in Lesterville Township. He is also listed in the Yankton County naturalization records as having received his final papers in 1883. By 1910 the township and range map for Odessa Township shows that **Wilhelm Mueller** had purchased Blessing's land.

Bohrer
Johannes Bohrer
Johannes Bohrer, 33, lived on the northwest quarter of section 3 along with his wife **Katharina**, 30, and seven-year-old son Peter. The "Neusatz Birth Records, 184x" state that Johannes was born on 5 December 1846 in Friedenthal, Crimea. His parents were **Martin** and **Philippine Theilaker Bohrer**. His brothers **Jacob** and **Joseph Bohrer** lived across the road in Hutchinson County. Jacob had a quarter section of homestead land that ran north and south in section 33 of Sweet Township. Joseph had homestead land in the southwest

quarter of 34 in Sweet Township next to Wilhelm Mueller's homestead.

The 1910 township and range map shows that **Gottlieb Schempp** owned at least 80 acres of the original homestead land.

Dux
August Dux

Sources do not offer much information about **August Dux** of the southeast quarter of section 26. An August Dux is recorded in the "Bessarabian Village Birth Records, 185x." This file states that he was born 13 August 1855 in Arzis, Bessarabia to **Michael** and **Henrietha Wendschlaag**. He is not listed in the 1880 U.S. Federal Census for Yankton County. But naturalization records show that he was born in 1855 in Russia and came to America in 1876. Dux applied for his naturalization papers on 12 September 1877.

By 1910 the township and range map shows that **Jacob M. Diede** and **Rosina Engel**, wife of Johann George Engel, owned different halves of Dux's land.

Engel
Johann Engel

Johann Engel was born in 1817 at Alt-Danzig, South Russia. On 10 May 1838 he married **Elizabeth Berndt** who was born in Alt-Danzig, circa 1818.

In 1873 Johann and Elizabeth immigrated to America on the ship *Westphalia*.[1] They homesteaded on the eastern and southeastern parts of section 14 and the northeastern quarter of section 23 in Odessa Township, Yankton County, Dakota Territory. Most of Johann Engel's daughters and their husbands, as well as son Johannes George Engel, homesteaded in Odessa Township.

Johann Engel helped organize the Hoffnung Reformed Church. He died 4 April 1889, and is buried in the Hoffnung Reformed Cemetery. Elizabeth Berndt Engel died in 1896 and is also buried in the Hoffnung Reformed Cemetery.

---

[1] *Heritage Review*, Bismarck, North Dakota: Germans from Russia Heritage Society, Volumes 5 and 6, June 1973, p. 42.

Johann Engel's land

The Hoffnung Cemetery

Many of their children were born in Russia, settled, and participated in the history of Odessa Township.

1. Barbara m Alexander Herrmann*
2. Katherina m Michael Serr*
3. Marie m Carl M. Ziegele*
4. Jacob b 1 June 1867 in Neu Danzig d 3 Sep 1867 in Gnadenfeld
5. Rosina m Friedrich Frank*
6. Johanna m George Jasmann*
7. Fredericka m W. Wilhelm Mueller*
8. Johannes George m Rosina Sayler
9. Philip m Carolina Suess

wives included in husband's histories

Philip H. Engel was born 6 January 1863, in Alt-Danzig, South Russia. He was 11 when he came to America with his family aboard the ship *Westphalia*.[1]

Philip married **Carolina Suess**, daughter of **Christoph** and **Rosina Koch Suess** who was also born in Russia. The Engel family homesteaded five miles south of Scotland, on section 14, in Lincoln Township, Bon Homme County, Dakota Territory.

Philip Engel's name is on the founder's list for the Hoffnung Reformed Church located on section 25, as well as the 1881 founders' list for the German Reformed Odessa Church built on section 31.

He worked in real estate and insurance in Scotland, South Dakota. Philip and Carolina Suess Engel's children were as follows:

1. Augustus Wilhelm b 19 September 1883, m Helena Drefs, 6 April 1911, d 1950, buried in Rosehill Cemetery, Scotland, SD
2. Elizabeth b August 1890, m Albert Peterson 12 June 1919, d 1928, tuberculosis, buried in Rosehill Cemetery, Scotland, SD
3. Emil Robert b 25 September 1894, m Emma Hellwig 11 January 1917, d 2 December 1967 of cancer, buried Rosehill Cemetery, Scotland, SD

---

[1] *Heritage Review*, Bismarck, North Dakota: Germans from Russia Heritage Society, Volumes 5 and 6, June 1973, p. 42.

Phillip and Carolina Suess Engel divorced. He later married a **Mrs. Mitchell**. Phillip died 15 November 1944.

Johannes George Engel

Johannes George Engel was born about 1859, in Alt-Danzig, South Russia, to **Johann** and **Elizabeth Berndt Engel**. Engel homesteaded on much of the central, southern, and western parts of section 14 in Odessa Township. He married **Rosina Sayler (Sailer)**, 16 March 1881. Born 12 March 1862, in Johannestal, Rosina was the daughter of **Ludwig** and **Fredericka Heinle Sayler** who also homesteaded in Odessa Township.

Johannes George Engel was a founder of the Hoffnung Reformed Church. Johannes George and Rosina Engel's children were:

1. Edward b 10 December 1881, Odessa Township
2. Lydia b 19 September 1883, Odessa Township, d 10 July 1893, buried Hoffnung Reformed Cemetery
3. Rosina b 19 September 1883, Odessa Township, d 1885, buried Hoffnung Reformed Cemetery (Lydia and Rosina were possibly twins)
4. August b 8 July 1885, Odessa Township, d 6 July 1893, buried Hoffnung Reformed Cemetery
5. Julius b 19 February 1887, Odessa Township, graduated from commercial college, Sioux City, Iowa, m Violet Benedict 17 June 1908, elected county auditor 1911, identified with Yankton Realty Company, Inc.
6. Bertha b February 1890, Odessa Township, m Frederick Saeger 28 November 1912
7. Johanna Rose b June 1892, Odessa Township
8. John G. b December 1894
9. Martha b 5 January 1897, d 15 September 1897, buried Hoffnung Reformed Cemetery
10. Sarah b 5 January 1897, d 13 September 1897, buried Hoffnung Reformed Cemetery
11. Rosina b 6 July 1898
12. Etna E. b 21 January 1903
13. Alvin b 1908

A notice dated 12 November 1885 from the land office at Yankton, Dakota Territory states that on 10 October 1885 a "notion of intention" to make "final proof of claim" was given to Johannes George Engel in Township 96, Range 57.

In 1893 Johannes George Engel retired from farming. He became postmaster in Lesterville, South Dakota. Around 1911 he moved his family to Scotland, Bon Homme County, South Dakota, where he worked in real estate.

Lesterville Ledger, 11 October 1918:

> *John Engel was in town and closed up a deal for the sale of his 80 acres farm NE of town to J. Walsh for $80.00 per acre.*

Frank
Andreas Frank

Andreas (Andrew) Frank, second son of Gottlieb and Katherina Koschel Frank, was born 27 March 1855 in South Russia.[1] He left Waterloo, South Russia, traveled to Hamburg, Germany, and finally sailed to America aboard the *Frisia* on 6 April 1874. Andreas applied for citizenship at Yankton, Dakota Territory, on 27 July 1874 and settled on part of the western half of section 25 in Odessa Township.

On 24 October 1875, Andreas married Magdalena Freier at the Odessa Lutheran Church. According to the 1850 Freudental birth records, Magdalena was the daughter of Johann Justinus and Maria Eva Geier Freier. She was born 6 June 1857 in Giderim, South Russia.

Mathias and Ludwig Sayler (Sailer, Saylor), other residents of Odessa Township, were "proof of homestead" witnesses for Andreas Frank. Mathias "Sailer" stated on the "Homestead Proof-Testimony of Proof" affidavit that he and Andrew had been friends since childhood. Andreas built an 18 x 32 stone house, 24 x 18 stable, and a 20 x 18 granary.

---

[1] Odessa Digital Library, St. Petersburg Archives, Rohrbach Birth Records, 185x (D. Wahl). http://pixel.cs.vt.edu/library/stpete/rohr/link/rohr185b.txt.

[4—348.]

No. 1.–HOMESTEAD.

Land Office at *Yankton, D.T.*

*September 27, 188*3.

I, Andreas Frank, of Lesterville P.O. Dak.
who made Homestead Application No. 3988 *for the*
North East ¼ 26 - 96 - 57

*claim to the land above described, and that I expect to prove my residence
and cultivation before Register or Receiver
at Yankton, Dak on Tuesday, Nov. 20, 1883,
by two of the following witnesses:*

Ludwig Sayler , ✗
Alexander Herrmann , ✗
Karl Ziegele , ✗
Michael Serr all, *of Lesterville P.O. Yankton Co. D.T.*

Andreas Frank
(Signature of claimant.)

Land Office at *Yankton, D.T.*

*September 27, 188*3.

*Notice of the above application will be published in the Press & Dak.
printed at Yankton, D.T. , which I hereby designate as the
newspaper published nearest the land described in said application.*

Jaweiter
Register.

STEASO-L.

Notice to Claimant.—Give time and place of proving up and name and title of the officer before whom proof is to be made; also
give names and post-offic ldress of four neighbors, two of whom must appear as your witnesses.
[10,357—76 M.]

*Andreas Frank's Homestead Application, dated September 27,
1883. His witnesses were Ludwig Sayler, Alexander Herrmann,
Karl Ziegele, and Michael Serr.*

Later Andreas applied for another 160 acres on section 26 which became his tree claim. In 1890 a neighbor, **Peter Sieler**, age 37, stated on the Timber Culture certifcate that he had known Andreas since 1874. He also stated that he had witnessed at least 1000 cottonwood, box elder, and acacia trees being planted, and they had grown to 20 to 25 feet high and 12" to 20" in diameter.

By 1910 he had purchased much of section 25. He also owned the northwest to southwest strip of section 30 in Jamesville Township that ran adjacent to his land in Odessa Township.

Andreas and Magdalena's children were all born in Odessa Township:

1. Emmanuel b 16 August 1876, m Salomine Radke, d 8 February 1937
2. Pauline b 4 April 1878, m ____ Mettler
3. Edward b 19 January 1880, m Louise Stern, d 4 March 1920, buried Odessa Lutheran Church Cemetery
4. Wilhelmina b 9 March 1881, m Stephen Stern 7 March 1901, d 25 April 1974, buried Unity Lutheran Cemetery, Freeman, SD
5. Christ b 27 March 1883, m Jacobina Schmidtgall 7 December 1905, d 5 May 1948, buried Pocatello, ID
6. Helena b 4 May 1885, m Johann George Frank 1901, d 18 February 1957, buried Sioux City, Iowa
7. Emil b 31 January 1887, d 15 September 1947
8. Theodore b 20 October 1889, m Amelia Stern, d 21 August 1937
9. Bertha b 24 September 1891, d infancy
10. Philip b 27 December 1892, d 20 February 1963, car accident
11. Laura b 7 April 1894, d infancy
12. Richard b 17 April 1895, d infancy
13. Lydia Maria Magdalena b 30 October 1896, m1 ____ Schumk; d 26 June 1926

Magdalena Freier Frank died Saturday, 8 December 1917 from diabetes and gangrene.

The Scotland Journal states:

> ### DIED
> *Mrs. Andrew Frank, age 60 years, 5 mons.[sic], and 13 days old, after a lingering illness of several months, died at her home Sunday. The funeral services were held at the German Congregational Church Wednesday forenoon [and were] conducted by Rev. Ruder. Besides the husband, deceased is survived by ten children, six sons and four daughters.*

Andreas died 15 September 1924. Both he and Magdalena are buried in the Rosehill Cemetery in Scotland, South Dakota.

Friedrich Frank Sr.

Friedrich Frank Sr., the oldest living son of **Gottlieb** and **Katherina Koschel Frank** known to come to America, was born in South Russia on 25 April 1849.

Friedrich, his wife **Rosina Engel Frank**, and their six-year-old daughter Rosina left Waterloo, South Russia, and traveled to Hamburg, Germany. On 6 April 1874, the family sailed to America aboard the *Frisia*. Friedrich's naturalization papers state that he arrived in May of 1874 at the Port of New York.

Rosina Engel Frank, the daughter of **Johann** and **Elizabeth Berndt Engel**, was born in Neu-Danzig, South Russia, in 1852.

In September 1876 Friedrich and Rosina settled on their homestead, section 26 in Odessa Township. The "Homestead Proof-Testimony of Witness" states that the couple had one daughter (Elizabeth) at the time. (Apparently the child Rosina who came to America with them died because she was never mentioned in a family listing.) The document also states that the Franks had an 18 x 30 concrete house, an 18 x 30 stone stable, and a 70 x 30 sheep stable. Friedrich dug a well and broke 80 acres of virgin soil. He valued the homestead at approximately $500. Although now abandoned, the homestead still stands in a cow pasture.

In addition to his homestead, Friedrich also had an additional 80 acres of land, allowed under the Timber Culture Act. According to the certifcate concerning section 15, Friedrich planted "at least 1100 cottonwood and black walnut trees on each of the six acres" for a total of 8840 trees. The *1910 Yankton County Atlas* shows that before Friedrich died that same year, he owned 320 acres to the west of the original homestead on the northern half of section 27.

Amelia Weidenbach, one of the first Frank family researchers, stated that Friedrich was a tall, heavy-set man. In addition to being a farmer, he was a skilled carpenter and cabinet-maker.[1] Friedrich helped organize the Hoffnung Reformed Church that was established 15 November 1882. Later, during the WPA period and under the South Dakota Graves Registration Project, the abandoned cemetery of the Hoffnung Reformed Church was also referred to as the Frank Cemetery in honor of Friedrich's son Wilhelm who served in World War I and is the only veteran buried there.

Friedrich Frank's Homestead in section 26.

[1] Amelia Weidenbach. Letters to author. 1990-1996.

p3v6'18

UNITED STATES OF AMERICA.

TERRITORY OF DAKOTA, } ss.

COUNTY OF YANKTON,

Second Judicial District.

before the subscriber, the Clerk of the United States District Court in and for the Second Judicial District, Territory of Dakota, being a Court of Record, and made oath that he was born in _Prussia_ _____ on or about the year eighteen hundred and _forty-seven_ _____; that he emigrated to the United States and landed at the Port of _New York_ _____ on or about the month of _May_ _____ in the year eighteen hundred and _seventy-four_ _____ that it is his bona fide intention to become A CITIZEN OF THE UNITED STATES, and to renounce forever all allegiance and fidelity to any foreign Prince, Potentate, State or Sovereignty whatsoever, and particularly to _Emperor of Prussia_ _____ whereof he is a subject.

Friedrich Frank _____ personally appeared

Friedrich Frank

Subscribed and sworn to before me, this _13th_
day of _May_ _____ A. D. 1874

_____ Clerk.

Friedrich Frank's Application for Naturalization.

[4—348.]

No. 1.—HOMESTEAD.

Land Office at Yankton, D.T.

Sept. 16, 1882.

I, *Friedrich Frank* of *Lesterville, D.T.* who made *Homestead Application No.* 1293 *for the* North West 26-96-57 *do hereby give notice of my intention to make final proof to establish my claim to the land above described, and that I expect to prove my residence and cultivation before* Register or Receiver *at* Yankton, Dak *on* Monday, Oct. 23, 1882, 10 a.m. *by two of the following witnesses:*

Alexander Herrmann, of ____
Ludwig Sailer, of ____
Jakob Kost, of ____
Mathias Sailer   all, of Lesterville, D.T.

Friedrich Frank
(Signature of claimant.)

Land Office at Yankton, D.T.

Sept. 16, 1882.

Notice of the above application will be published in the Press & Dak *printed at* Yankton, Dak, *which I hereby designate as the newspaper published nearest the land described in said application.*

STEREO'S.

____ G. Awette
Register.

Notice to Claimant.—Give time and place of proving up and name and date of the officer before whom proof is to be made; also give names and post-office address of four neighbors, two of whom must appear as your witnesses.
[9085—40,000.]

Friedrich Frank's Homestead Application, dated September 16, 1882. His witnesses were Alexander Herrmann, Ludwig Sailer, Jakob Kost and Mathias Sailer.

(4—196.)

HOMESTEAD.

Land Office at *Yankton, Dak*

October 23, 1882

FINAL CERTIFICATE.
No. *2126*

APPLICATION,
No. *1293*

It is hereby certified That, pursuant to the provisions of Section No. 2291, Revised Statutes of the United States, *Friedrich Frank* of *Yankton Co. Dak.* has made payment in full for

North West quarter

of Section No. *Twenty six* (26), in Township No. *Ninety Six* (96 north) of Range No. *Fifty three* (53 west), of the .... *5* .... Principal Meridian ...., containing .... *160* 100 acres.

Now, therefore, be it known, That on presentation of this Certificate to the COMMISSIONER OF THE GENERAL LAND OFFICE, the said *Friedrich Frank* shall be entitled to a Patent for the Tract of Land above described.

Register.

ELECTRO'S

[9866—15,000.]

Final Homestead Certificate granted to Friedrich Frank
on October 23, 1882.

Elizabeth Frank, died of tuberculosis in 1890

W. G. Gibbon,

SCOTLAND,
SOUTH DAKOT

Carolina Frank, died of tuberculosis in 1892

On 26 July 1890, the Frank family members began dying of tuberculosis. Elizabeth, the oldest living daughter, was the first to die. The second oldest child, Carolina, died two years later in 1892. On 13 September 1896, wife and mother Rosina also died. *The Scotland Journal*, 19 September 1896, states her death but not the cause:

> *Mrs. Frank, a lady residing near Lesterville on Sunday last died and was buried Tuesday, Rev. Treik officiating.*

Friedrich Frank served from 1895-1896 as a director for the Southern South Dakota Fair Association.

The Scotland Journal, 16 March 1895 states:

> *A called meeting of the stock holders of the Southern South Dakota Fair Association was held here Wednesday in the City Hall for the purpose of electing eleven directors for the considering year. Fredreck [sic] Frank for Yankton County (those present were unanimously in favor of holding a fair the coming fall).*

Children of Friedrich and Rosina Frank:
1. Rosina b 1868, Waterloo, SR, d Odessa Township.
2. Elizabeth b 14 February 1875, Odessa Township, d 26 July 1890 of tuberculosis, buried Hoffnung Reformed Cemetery
3. Carolina b 23 February 1877, Odessa Township, d 1 May 1892 of tuberculosis, buried Hoffnung Reformed Cemetery
4. Johann George b 19 April 1880, Odessa Township, m Helena Frank, d 18 January 1946, buried Sioux City, Iowa
5. Frederich Jr. b 9 April 1882, Odessa Township, m 17 December 1907, Scotland, Anna Maria Hauck, d 21 February 1920 of pulmonary pneumonia, buried Hoffnung Reformed Cemetery
6. Albert b 1 March 1884, Odessa Township, d 5 February 1928, buried Menno, SD, m 26 May 1908, Lesterville, Paulina Gimbel, (b 28 January 1891, d 1 Sept 1980)

7. Rosina b 24 March 1886, Odessa Township, m 1 March 1911, Scotland, Richard Weidenbach, d 5 August 1917 of tuberculosis, buried Rosehill Cemetery, Scotland, SD.
8. Solomon b 24 September 1888, Odessa Township, d 7 May 1915 of tuberculosis, buried Hoffnung Reformed Cemetery
9. William F. b 24 September 1890, Odessa Township, d 14 February 1927, buried Hoffnung Reformed Cemetery

Friedrich remarried. Court records from McIntosh County, North Dakota, state the following about the marriage that was held in the Reformed Church:

> *Fredrich Frank, Lesterville, SD and Loisa Boettcher, Kassel, ND m July 14, 1897 by H.W. Stienecker; w. (witnesses) John Isaak-John Schaeffer.*[1]

Louisa Berndt Boettcher Frank (spelling and pronunciation variation: Bettger, Bottcher, Boettcher) was born 6 September 1850 in New Danzig, South Russia. Her father **Friedrich Berndt** was born circa 1827 in Alt-Danzig, South Russia. Her mother, **Elizabeth Boettcher**, was born in Alt-Danzig, South Russia, circa 1827.

Curt Renz, who has researched the Engel, Berndt, and Boettcher families extensively, shows the following children belong to **Friedrich Berndt and Elizabeth Boettcher (Bettger) Berndt**:

1. Louisa
2. Jakob b 4 November 1853 m Rosina Edinger
3. Friedrich b 28 July 1861 m Maria Herrlich
4. Johann b 4 June 1865 m1 Dorothea Klein, m2 Christina Munsch
5. Katherine b 20 September 1866 m Andrew Kluck
6. Wilhelmina m Michael Redinger
7. Elisabeth m _____ Wagner
8. Karl

---

[1] *Heritage Review*, "Marriage Records 1890-1903 McIntosh County, North Dakota," Bismarck, North Dakota: Germans from Russia Heritage Society, February 1983, Volume 13, No.1, p. 5.

Friedrich Frank and his second wife, Louisa Berndt Boettcher Frank

Karl Stumpp validates Renz' research that Louisa's mother **Elizabeth Boettcher Berndt's** parents were **Georg** and **Luise Boettcher**. The Boettcher family arrived at Waterloo, South Russia, in 1832. Their children were as follows:

1. Martin 21 years   5. Gottlieb 10 years
2. Johann 16 years   6. Ludwig 4 years
3. Friedrich 14 years   7. Elisabetha 5 years
4. Christoph 12 years

Renz also shows that Louisa's first marriage was to **Johann Boettcher** who was born 21 January 1848 in Waterloo, South Russia. Johann, Louisa Boettcher and their children emigrated to the United States in 1893. Johann died at Herried, South Dakota, 22 December 1896. On 14 July 1897, Louisa Boettcher married Friedrich Frank in McIntosh County, North Dakota.

Friedrich and Louisa Berndt Frank

Gottlieb Frank Sr.'s land on left — right the remains of Friedrick Frank's tree claim.

Fried. Frank's Homestead

Gottlieb Frank Sr. (on right).

Gottlieb Frank Sr., 1820-1878

The 1900 U.S. Federal Census for Yankton County states that Louisa was 49 and born in 1850. She and Friedrich Frank had been married for two years. She was the mother of five children, but only three were still living. According to the census, she had the following children living with her and the Frank family:

Bettger, Karl, 16, born January 1884, immigrated in 1893, and occupation farm laborer; Bettger, Friedrick, 8, born November 1891, and immigrated in 1893.

Sometime after 1900, Louisa and Friedrich were separated. On 13 January 1911 Friedrich Frank died. The 21 January 1911 *Scotland Journal* states:

> **Fred Frank, aged 62 years old, after a year's illness passed away at his home in the south part of Scotland at 11 o'clock Friday afternoon; his death being attributed to dropsy and paralysis of the heart.**
>
> **The funeral was held Sunday and services [were] conducted by Rev. Treick, pastor of the Scotland Reformed church, in the Reformed Church thirteen miles southeast of town, and the remains interred in the church cemetery there besides those of wife and two daughters.**
>
> **The deceased is survived by five children: George, Albert, William, Solomon and Rosa Frank.[1]**

According to Bon Homme County Probate Court records, Friederich Frank had paid Louisa $1500 "in full settlement of all matters relative to her rights in the marriage relation." He bequeathed to his sons George, Frederick Jr., Solomon, Albert and Wilhelm and his "beloved daughter, Rosina Frank, equal parts and shares [of] the following described real property." Friederich also willed to his children the south half of the southeast quarter of section 15, the north half of section 27, and the northwest quarter of section 26 of Odessa Township, Yankton County. In addition, he also left to them his lot and house in the city of Scotland, SD, "Lot Two (2) in Block Two (2) in that part of the city of Scotland known

---

[1] The article neglects to mention Frederich Frank Jr.

and platted as South Scotland (my said sons and daughter shall hold the same as tenants in common share and share alike.)"

The last will and testament of Friederich Frank states that his brother-in-law **Philip Engel** was the executor of his estate. In addition, he willed "...four shares at $25.00 each in the Menno Lumber Company; one note on Frederich Frank, in the sum of $275.00..."

After the Franks separated, Louisa went to live at Herried, South Dakota, with her son **Carl Bettger** who was in the dairy and poultry business. She visited her daughter **Paulina Pudwill** (Mrs. Henry Pudwill) who lived north of town across the border in North Dakota. She had been there for three weeks when she began to experience numbness in her leg. Except for the slight attack of paralysis, she seemed to be managing well until one evening while she was visiting with family members, she doubled over from an apparent heart attack. Louisa Bettger died 1 December 1930; she was 80 years old. The funeral services were conducted from the Herried Baptist Church and she was buried in the Fairview Cemetery in Herried, South Dakota.

Gottlieb Frank Jr.

Gottlieb Frank Jr. was born 3 October 1862, in South Russia. In September 1874, when he was 12, he came to America with his parents **Gottlieb** and **Katherina Koschel Frank.**

On 25 November 1880, at the age of 18, Gottlieb married his neighbor **Christina Horst**. Born 28 August 1864 in Worms, South Russia, Christina was the daughter of **Johann** and **Katharine Muehlbeier Horst** who homesteaded on section 15.

After the deaths of Gottlieb Jr.'s parents, and at the time of the final proving up of his father's homestead, brothers Friedrich and Andreas, as legal heirs of their father's estate, signed the land title over to Gottlieb Jr. On 4 May 1882, Gottlieb applied for naturalization, and on 14 March 1884, he took his final oath of allegiance. The children of Gottlieb and Christina were:

1. Johanna b 29 June 1884 or 27 June 1885, Dakota Territory, confirmed Worms, SD, 12 March 1899, d 29 July 1954, m1 Chris Mettler 20 December 1902 (b 20 December 1882), m2 Malvey Almire

2. Henry b 7 October 1888, Dakota Territory, d 22 May or June 1952 Ronneby, MN, m Annie Hieska Rodewald 24 December 1914, (b 21 August 1892 Germany, d 9 July 1985/6 Ronneby, MN)

3. Christina b 5 January 1891, SD, d 19 March 1972 Rapid City, SD, m Theodore Buxcel 20 March 1909 (b 2 November 1877, d 26 May 1967 Rapid City, SD)

Christine Horst Frank died 24 Jan 1891.

On 21 June 1891, Gottlieb married **Elizabeth Theurer** who was born circa 1873. She came to America in 1875. The 1900 U.S. Federal Census states that Elizabeth Theurer Frank was on her second marriage and had had eight children of which only six were still living.

Elizabeth Theurer Frank, second wife of Gottlieb Frank Jr.

Gottlieb Frank Jr. and Elizabeth had the following children:

1. Julius b 21 April 1892, m widow Bertha Orth, d 18 October 1954
2. Herbert b 1895, d 13 April 1898, Worms, SD
3. Theophiel (Taft) b 2 November 1896, Worms, SD, bap 11 July 1897, d 21 February 1985, m 15 April 1917 Martha Orth (b 22 October 1893, d 11 December 1989, buried Rosehill Cemetery, Scotland, SD, dau/o William and Margaret nee Schmidt Orth)
4. Lea Magdalena b 13 August 1898 Worms, SD, bap 2 October 1898, m 10 September 1921 John H. Magstadt at Scotland, SD. Lea d 13 July 1977, buried Joshua Memorial Park Cemetery, Lancaster, CA
5. Herbert Emil b 23 January 1901, Menno, SD, bap 31 March 1901, d 11 March 1980, m Ida M. Gillette (b 29 March 1901)
6. Rheinhold b 27 March 1902 Worms, SD, d 5 August 1965, m Ella Hauck 9 June 1927 (b 26 March 1906)
7. Albert, m1 ____ Guthmuller; m2 Caroline Vilhauer 28 December 1926 (b 15 July 1904)

Gottlieb died 31 March 1918 from gastric carcinoma, or stomach cancer. He was 55 years, 5 months, 28 days old.

Gottlieb Frank Sr.

According to the *Waterloo, Beresan District Odessa, 1858 Census*, **Gottlieb Frank** (2) was born in South Russia in 1825. Gottlieb's father, **Gottlieb Frank** (1) is listed in the St. Petersburg Rohrbach 1860 death records as being born 6 March 1777 in Bernek, Wuerttemberg, and dying 1 January 1864 in Waterloo, South Russia. He married **Katharina Herz** who is also listed in the St. Petersburg Archives. She died in Waterloo, SR, 5 September 1838 at 42 years of age.

The St. Petersburg archives indicate Gottlieb (1) and Katharina Herz Frank had the following children:

1. Jacob Heinrich Frank, b 1820 in Waterloo; d 20 July 1848 in Waterloo, SR, m Christina Grotz October 1842 in Rohrbach, SR

2. Friedrich Frank, b 27 June 1822 in Waterloo; d 19 July 1855 in Waterloo, SR, m Bertha Hoeffle October 1842 in Rohrbach, SR
3. Gottlieb Christian, b 1825, Waterloo; d 20 December 1878 in Yankton, SD., m Catharina Koschel 18 September 1844 in Johannesthal, SR; d 22 March 1879 in Lesterville, SD (see biography)*
4. Maria Magdalena Frank, b 2 September 1834 in Waterloo, SR, m Andeas Bellon 2 November 1854
5. Anna Frank, b 2 September 1834 in Waterloo, SR, m Gottlieb Gross 1 December 1851. They had the following children: Katharina Magdalina b 25 August 1854 d 23 Feb 1856; Elizabetha b 24 May 1856; Christina b 25 July 1858; Catharina b 4 August 1860; Friederike Helene b 27 April 1862; Rosine Friederike b 8 November 1864 –(All born in Waterloo)
6. Wilhelm Frank, b December 1841 in Waterloo, SR, d 30 June 1842 in Waterloo, SR

Gottlieb Frank (2) married **Catharina Koschel** 19 September 1844. The 1828 census for "Colonie Klein-Freudental" in *the Neu-Freudental, Liebental District Odessa, 1858 Census* indicates that Catharina was born circa 1825 to **Jacob** and **(Anna) Maria Agnesia Koschel**. The death records for the elder Koschels state that Jacob was born in 1797 and Anna Maria Agnesia was born 3 January 1799 in Klein Sachsenheim, Germany. Anna Maria Agnesia's parents were **Johannes** and **Agnesia Bauer Weber**. Johannes was born circa 1778 and Agnesia was born circa 1777.

The 1840 St. Petersburg marriage records for Rohrbach state that the couple was from Johannestal and Waterloo. Between May and September 1874, the Franks and three sons and daughter-in-law, Friedrich and Rosina, Andreas, and Gottlieb Jr., arrived in America from Waterloo, South Russia. Gottlieb Sr.'s naturalization application states that he arrived at the Port of New York in September 1874. He applied for naturalization on 9 October 1874 in Yankton County. He then homesteaded on the northeast quarter of section 22 in Odessa Township.

According to *The Daily Press and Dakotan*, 20 December 1878:

Suddenly Taken Away
Gottlieb Frank Dies from Heart Disease
in the Office of Morgan's Elevator

A Russian named Gottlieb Frank, residing at Odessa, in this county died suddenly in the office of Morgan's elevator, between two and three o'clock this afternoon. He had brought a load of wheat to town, and sold it to Morgan. After unloading it at the elevator he got down from the wagon, and as he reached the ground he placed his hands on his chest and remarked that he felt a severe pain there. He then walked into the office to receive pay for his wheat, and stood a few moments at the desk while a check was drawn for him. Receiving the check he turned to depart and fell to the floor. In a few moments Mr. Frank was dead. The deceased was a German-Russian who had been a resident of Dakota only a few years.

HOMESTEAD.

APPLICATION ⎰
No. *11.5.2.* ⎱   **Land Office at** *Gaurlw as*

Nrverhu 26, 187*5*. —

I, *Gottlieb Frank*, of *Gaurlui-Co
D.J* . do hereby apply to enter, under the provisions
of the act of Congress approved May 20, 1862, entitled "An Act to secure
homesteads to actual settlers on the public domain," the *Nort East-
1/4* of Section *2 2* in Township *9.6* . of
Range *57*, containing *160* acres.

Gottlint Frrnrk

Land Office at *Gaurlu as*

Nrvauhu 26, 1875. —

I. *Aurhhing*, **REGISTER OF THE LAND OFFICE**,
do hereby certify that the above application is for Surveyed Lands of the
class which the applicant is legally entitled to enter under the Homestead
act of May 20, 1862, and that there is no prior, valid, adverse right to the
same.

Aurhhing
Register.

Gottlieb Frank's Homestead Application, dated November 26, 1875.

Shortly after Gottlieb's death, on 22 March 1879, Catharina also died. Both individuals are supposedly buried in the Odessa Reformed Church Cemetery.

Because it took approximately five years to "prove up" on a homestead and eight years to become naturalized, Gottlieb Frank died before he was able to realize either event. The "Homestead Proof Testimony of Witness" form of the Homestead Application declares that Gottlieb Frank's occupation was "farmer" and he resided in Yankton County, Dakota Territory. After he declared his intentions to become a citizen, he settled upon his homestead on 26 November 1875. He built a 35 x 22 concrete house, a 28 x 18 stable, 24 x 22 granary and dug a well. Also by the time he settled, he had broken 60 acres of sod. The total value of his residence was valued to be about $600.

The following children belong to Gottlieb and Catharina Koschel Frank:

1. Jacob b 23 May 1845 Waterloo d 18 Jan 1847
2. Johann Georg b 7 Jul 1847 Waterloo
3. Friedrich b 25 April 1849, m Rosina Engel*
4. Wilhelm b 4 Jun 1851 Waterloo, d 18 Nov 1905 Garrison, ND, m Johanna Wuest b 16 June 1852 Rohrbach, d 26 October 1934, Garrison, ND
5. Katharina 19 Feb 1853 Waterloo could have possibly married Christian Grotz 27 September 1877
6. Andreas Frank b 27 Mar 1855 Waterloo, m Magdalena Freier (b 24 October 1853)*
7. Magdalena b 13 Mar 1857 Waterloo d 16 Mar 1857 Waterloo
8. Elisabethe b 7 Sep 1858 Waterloo d 23 Feb 1865 (6 yrs 11 mos 8 days) Waterloo, b in Gobasch
9. Gottlieb b 15 Dec 1860 Waterloo d 8 Sep 1861 (8 months 24 days)
10. Gottlieb Jr. b 3 October 1862, m1 Christina Horst, m2 Elizabeth Theurer
11. Peter b 2 Jan 1865 Waterloo d 28 Nov 1867 Waterloo 3 yrs., b Janskino
12. son b 3 21 Dec 1866, Waterloo—stillborn—Born in Janschina

Freimark
Ernst Freimark

Ernst Freimark, his wife **Elisabeth Fischer Freimark**, and their two young children, Friedrich and newborn Daniel, arrived in America 13 November 1876 aboard the *S. S. Berlin*. Friedrich was born 17 June 1875 and Daniel was born 25 July 1876 in Danielsfeld. The Freimark family homesteaded on the northeast quarter of section 27.

The following are some of Ernst and Elisabeth Freimark's other children:

1. Gottlieb b 21 March 1882, bap 7 May 1882
2. Anna Magdalena b 2 September 1883, bap 27 October 1883
3. Catherina b 30 April 1885, bap 31 May 1885

Freier
Christian Freier

Christian Freier was born 28 April 1853. His parents were **Johann Justinus** and **Eva Maria Gaier Freier** from Freudental, South Russia. *The Freudental, Liebental District Odessa, 1861-1880, Church FB* records show that Johann and Eva Maria married in 1850. The records also show the following children born in Freudental:

1. Christian b 8 April 1853
2. Catharine b 5 May 1855
3. Magdalene b 13 July 1857
4. Philip b 19 August 1859

Christian lived on section 18. According to the land office records listed in *The Dakota Citizen*, 6 June 1884:

[Freier]...filed notice of his intention to make final proof in support of his claim under his homestead No. 3187, for lots 2 and 3 and east half of southwest quarter of section 18, township 96, range 57. He names the following witnesses to prove his continuous residence upon and cultivation of said land viz: Heinrich Weidenbach, Jakob Auch, Peter Sieler and Nikolaus Jungmann, all of Scotland, Bon Homme County, Dakota.

Although the 1880 U.S. Federal Census for Yankton County shows that Christian's brother Phillip, 21, and wife Anna Maria, 18, lived in Odessa Township, Phillip is not one of the original homesteaders.

Hermann
Alexander Hermann

Alexander Hermann* (variations of spelling: Herman, Herrman, Herrmann) was born 6 July 1837 in Güldendorf, South Russia.[1] According to St. Petersburg Archives for 1830 birth records for Rohrbach, Alexander's parents were **Johannes** and **Eva Catharina Horst Hermann**. They were both born in Germany. The Horsts and the Hermanns left Germany and traveled to Russia where Johannes and Eva Catharina eventually met and married.[2]

On 30 December 1858 Alexander married **Barbara Engel**. Barbara was born in Alt-Danzig, South Russia, on 17 March 1838 to **Johann** and **Elizabeth Berndt Engel**. The Engel family also settled in Odessa Township.

On 6 April 1874, the Hermanns and their children boarded the ship *Frisia* at Hamburg, Germany. Along with the Hermanns, Barbara's sister Rosina Engel Frank, her husband Friedrich Frank, and the Frank's young daughter Rosina were also onboard. The ship list states the ages of the Hermann family members: Alexander 36, Barbara 35, Johannes 15, Sophie 9, Rosine 3, and Philipp 4 months. The passenger list also states that they were leaving Gnadenfeld, South Russia.

Alexander homesteaded on the southern half of section 23 in Odessa Township. He helped organize the farmers co-op which became the German Mutual Farmers Insurance Company of Bon Homme County, South Dakota. In 1881 he also helped organize the German Reformed Odessa Church.[3]

---

[1] *Heritage Review*, "Obituaries from the Dakota Freie Presse." Fargo, ND: Germans from Russia Heritage Society, 19:3 (Sept. 1989), p. 22.

[2] *Yankton County History*, Yankton County Historical Society, Yankton, South Dakota, and Curtis Media Corporation, Dallas, Texas, 1987, p. 472.

[3] Ibid.

In 1900 the Hermanns retired from farming and moved to Scotland, South Dakota, where Alexander died in March 1905. Barbara died 9 July 1921 of cardio-renal disease and complications of old age. Both are buried in the Rosehill Cemetery, Scotland, South Dakota. Their children are as follows:

1. Johann b 1 November 1859, Alt-Danzig, SR, m Amalia Mueller, d 12 June 1914
2. Sophia b 24 May 1868, Alt-Danzig, SR, m Albert Litz, d 1953
3. Rosina b 4 February 1870, Alt-Danzig, SR, m Emanuel Radak, d 16 May 1895
4. Emanuel b 24 November 1875, Odessa Township, m1 Rebecca Rathke; m2 Naomi Stippich, d 23 July 1962
5. August b 10 May 1877, Odessa Township, m Theresa Schmelzel, d 28 March 1900

Johann Hermann

Johann Hermann's homestead was part of the northern half of section 24. The son of **Alexander** and **Barbara Engel Hermann,** Johann was born 1 November 1859 in Neu-Danzig, South Russia.

Johann Hermann, 1859-1914

In 1882 Johann married **Amalia Mueller** who, according to St. Petersburg Archives—Neusatz, was born 4 May 1861 in Friedenthal, Crimea, South Russia. She was the daughter of **Joseph** and **Katerina Dorothea Bub Mueller** of sections 12 and 13, Lesterville Township, Yankton County. Amalia's parents, Katerina Bub, born 29 September 1827, and Joseph Mueller, born 12 July 1825, were married 1 February 1845 at Friedenthal, Crimea, South Russia.[1]

The Joseph Mueller family left Russia in 1875 and arrived in New York aboard the *S.S. Klopstock* on 7 July 1875. The vessel sailed from Hamburg, Germany. The ship list states the following were aboard:

Muller
Josef, 50, m, farmer
Catharina, 48, f, wife
Jacobine, 18, f, child
Paul, 16, m, child
Amelia, 12, f, child
Julie, 8, f, child
Josef, 6, m, child
Lydia, 5, f, child

For a number of years, Johann Hermann was Commissioner of Public Highways. In 1905-1906, he served in the South Dakota House of Representatives. Johann Hermann also helped organize the Hoffnung Reformed Church, section 34, Odessa Township. Along with his father Alexander Hermann, he helped organize the German Mutual Farmers' Insurance Company of Bon Homme County.

Johann and Amalia's children were as follows:

1. Robert P. b December 1882, m Emma Schempp of Menno, SD, d 1957 of cancer
2. Richard E. b April 1884, m Elizabeth Gimbel of Lesterville, SD, d 1945
3. Emanuel Herbert b February 1890, m Lillian Johanna Hauck in 1914, d 1969 of stroke; farmed Hermann homestead

---

[1] *Yankton County History*, pp. 471-472.

4. Alida R. b December 1893, m Arthur Winter in 1814, d 1978 in Lodi, CA, of a stroke
5. Susanna b June 1897, d 1920 of pneumonia

Johann Hermann died in 1914. Amalia Mueller Hermann then married **John Koth**. She died 22 February 1936. Both Johann and Amalia Hermann are buried at Menno, South Dakota.

Horst
Johann Horst

Johann Horst homesteaded on the southwest quarter of section 15. Although Yankton County naturalization records state that he was born in 1836, the *Worms, Beresan District Odessa, 1858 Census* shows that he is 22 at the time, the 1830 Rohrbach birth records indicate that he was born 11 February 1837 in Worms to **(Jakob) Friedrich** and **Barbara Bengert Horst**.

Karl Stumpp's *The Emigration from Germany to Russia in the Years 1763 to 1862* reveals Friedrich was 12 at the time of the Worms census taken in 1816, accounting for his birth to be circa 1804. The records also reveal that the Horst family arrived at Worms in 1809 (*the Worms, Beresan District Odessa, 1858 Census* verifies this). Georg Horst was 45 and came from Hoffenheim/Sinsheim-Baden with his wife Frau Maria who was also 45. They also had the following children with them: Ludwig 18, Jakob 16, Friedrich 12, Katharina 10, and step-children Karl Schept 13, from Helmsheim/Burchsal-Baden, Katharina Schept 16 and Georg 11.

The Rohrbach 1830 birth, marriage, and death records reveal Friedrich Horst's first wife to be **Anna Maria (Barbara) Bender** who died 21 December 1835. Friedrich and Anna Maria had a child, Catharina Salomea, born 12 Nov 1833 in Worms; she died 30 November 1835. Friedrich then married **Anna Maria (Barbara) Bengert** on 18 February 1836. If this information is true, the mother Barbara died 31 October 1838, an infant son, Ludwig, died 8 November 1838, and the father Friedrich died 16 December 1838, leaving Johann orphaned.

The 1850 marriage files for Rohrbach state that Johann Horst married **Catharine (Katherina) Muehlbeier** on 10 November 1857. The Rohrbach files also show that Catharine was born 12 Aug

1834 at Worms to **Tobias M.** and **Anna Maria Maas Muehlbeier**. Catharine was baptised 18 August 1834 in Rohrbach.

According to the ship list for the *Schiller*, the following Horst family members came to America from Worms, South Russia, 20 August 1874:

Johann, 39
Catherine, 41
Louisa, 16
Catherine, 14
Margretha, 8
Christina, 7
Friedrich, 3
Jacob, 9/12[1]

Johann Horst homesteaded on the southwest quarter of section 15. He applied for naturalization on 19 October 1874.

The 1880 U.S. Federal Census states that at the time, Horst was 43 and a farmer. He and both parents were born in Russia. His wife Katharine was 46, born in Russia, and both of her parents were born in Prussia.

Johann and Katharine's children are listed below:

1. Margareth 18
2. Christina 16 m Gottlieb Frank Jr., d 24 January 1891
3. Frederich 10
4. Jakob 8

Johann established the Horst Private Cemetery on his land and although the WPA records state that there are others buried on the land, he is the only one listed. The cemetery's general appearance is

"not very good, on gravel road to Menno N. No fence, ground on top of hill, was enclosed with barb-wire but this is all destroyed only one post remains and one rotten strand of wire. Holes dug in graves. It was organized by owner Mr. Johann Horst dead and buried

[1] Pritzkau, Gwen, "Passenger Lists." *Work Paper* No. 12, August 1973, American Historical Society of Germans from Russia, p. 61.

there. This cemetary [*sic*] dates back 65 or more years as informant stated and dug four family graves on this cemetary [*sic*]. It's not used today. All family moved away. Lost land."

Johann Horst was 68 years old when he died.

Jasmann
Christian Jasmann

Christian Jasmann, oldest son of George Jasmann Sr. and Elisabeth Weidenbach, was born 2 September 1848 in Worms.[1] Christian married Catharina Vaatz, 16 January 1869 in Worms.[2] Catharina was born in 20 April 1847 in Balditzki to August Christian Vaatz and Catharina Weist.[3] August Christian and Catharina Weist married 5 Mar 1846 in Rohrbach.[4]

The Christian Jasmann family left Russia in 1872 with other members of the Jasmann family. They sailed to America aboard the *Silesia*. With Christian and Catharina were their two daughters two-year-old Emma and nine-month-old Julie.

Christian Jasmann was one of the scouts who, in the spring of 1873, went looking for land on which the whole group of German immigrants from Russia could settle. He and others, including his father Georg Sr., brother Georg Jr., and Heinrich Stoller, were the first to arrive in Dakota. Christian Jasmann claimed the northeast quarter of section 33, and the northwest and southwest quarters of section 34.

According to the 1880 U.S. Federal Census, Christian Jasmann was a dry goods merchant in Scotland, Dakota Territory.

[1] Odessa Digital Library, St. Petersburg Archives, Rohrbach Birth Records, 184x (D. Wahl). http://pixel.cs.vt.edu/library/stpete/rohr/link/rohr184b.txt.

[2] Odessa Digital Library, St. Petersburg Archives, Rohrbach Marriage Records, 186x (D. Wahl). http://pixel.cs.vt.edu/library/stpete/rohr/link/rohr186m.txt.

[3] Odessa Digital Library, St. Petersburg Archives, Rohrbach Birth Records, 184x (D. Wahl). http://pixel.cs.vt.edu/library/stpete/rohr/link/rohr184b.txt.

[4] Odessa Digital Library, St. Petersburg Archives, Rohrbach Marriage Records, 184x (D. Wahl). http://pixel.cs.vt.edu/library/stpete/rohr/link/rohr184m.txt.

Christian and Catherine's children were:

1. Emma b 24 Feb 1870 d 4 Jan 1880
2. Juliane b 10 July 1871
3. Amalia Jasmann b 1876, m Imanuel Geist
4. Juliana Jasmann b 1877
5. Emilie Jasmann b 12 October 1878, teacher, m Harry Wright
6. Robert Jasmann b 17 April 1880, dentist
7. Wilhelmina Jasmann b 28 May 1882, teacher, m Chris Griess
8. Elsie (Eliza) Jasmann b 16 November 1886, teacher, m
   William Rodekin

Christian Jasmann was also an influential businessman in and
around Scotland, South Dakota. The *Scotland Citizen* had the
following to say about him:

> **23 May 1889** - C Jassman is shipping cattle and cows to Eureka,
> Dakota, for sale to new immigrants that are coming in there this
> spring
> *****
> **7 November 1889** - The commissioners election in this district
> Tuesday was spirited, although only a two-thirds vote was cast.
> C. Jasmann had accepted the nomination on both the democratic
> and republican tickets and it was not known until Monday that
> he would have any opposition when Joseph Janda came out an
> independent candidate and organized his canvas so well that he
> was elected by 14 majority. The vote stood: Janda 152; Jasmann
> 138. Mr Janda will make a good commissioner and being a
> democrat makes a majority of the county board democratic.
> *****
> **15 May 1890** - Under the order of business Christian Jassmann
> presented his application to the council for water supply for the
> store building corner of Main and 2nd street and occupied by
> Diehl and Hain as a drug store.
> *****
> **25 December 1890** - C Jasmann had the good fortune to strike a
> good market with his special train load of fat cattle shipped to
> Chicago last week, and realized considerable more than he had
> expected from the sale. A result that is as gratifying to all as to
> Mr. Jasmann, as it encourages the business in that line and gives
> our farmers a better market for their cattle and corn.

Scotland Journal for 28 August 1898 also states:

> **Christ Jasmann has threshed his winter wheat, and we
> understand it turned out thirty bushels to the acre.**

Christian died of dropsy on 12 July 1900 when he was 52. By
1910 **Jacob Mutschelknaus Jr.,** and **B. F. Freidel** owned Christian
Jasmann's land.

Georg Jasmann Jr.

Georg Jasmann Jr., born July 1852, in Worms, South Russia, came to America on the *Silesia* on 13 November 1872 with his father **Georg Fredrich Sr.**, stepmother **Katherina Diede Kusler Mueller** (?), and the rest of the Jasmann family.

After staying the winter in Ohio with his family and other friends, Georg Jasmann Jr. became one of the scouts sent out to find land for the first groups of German-Russians that arrived in America.

Georg Jasmann's homestead and tree claim covered the northeast quarter and the southeast quarter of section 28. On 10 November 1874, he married **Johanna Engel**, daughter of Johann and Elizabeth Engel. According to the 1880 U.S. Federal Census, Georg, Johanna, and daughter Lydia were living in Scotland, Bon Homme County, Dakota Territory. By 1910 **John L. Sayler** owned both quarters of the original homestead land.

Georg Jasmann owned Jasmann's Market in Scotland, located three doors west of the city post office.

The editor for *The Scotland Weekly Citizen*, later known as *The Scotland Citizen*, often wrote short commentaries about Georg Jasmann Jr. in its local section. Following are a few excerpts:

> **23 August 1888** - Geo. Jassman left Monday for Portland, Oregon, and other Pacific coast points to look the country over.
>
> *****
>
> **6 September 1888** - George Jassman returned yesterday from his trip to Portland, Oregon. He met there among other old Scotland people his brother, Dave Jasman, Fred Pfaff, E. Shupe, and F. Neubauer, who are all doing well and are well satisfied with their new homes. Mr. Jasmann thinks Oregon has a fine climate but is no place for a man to go without he has large means.
>
> *****
>
> **25 April 1889** - Boys and cigarettes are a dangerous combination. One day last fall a barn in back of the post office was discovered to be on fire also the ice house of Geo. Jassman near by set on fire. By the prompt action of citizens both fires were extinguished and the town saved

from a disastrous conflagration. These fires were undoubtedly set by boys playing with matches or smoking.
*****

4 July 1889 - Geo. Jassman, F. B. Morgan, H.A. Reeves and J.E. Zeebach attended the races at Mitchel last week.
*****

15 May 1890 - Geo Jasmann presented his application for water supply to be used in his meat market on Main St. for a water motor. On motion of Councilman Balach the application of Geo Jasmann was referred to the water works committee to report at an adjourned meeting as to terms to be paid to said city for said privileges as asked for in said application.
*****

26 June 1890 - George Jasmann has put in a water motor in his meat market to run his machinery.
*****

2 October 1890 - Among the corn palace visitors from Scotland Friday and Saturday were F. G. Hale and wife, Geo. Jasmann and wife...

Sometime before 1895, Georg Jasmann Jr. and his family moved to Portland, Oregon. Georg Jr. was listed in the Portland City Directory for 1895. It states that he was working in the dairy business at 948 Upshur. He also resided at the same residence.

By 1900, the Georg Jasmann Jr. family was in the state census for Portland City, Multonomah County, and living in Precinct 48, on Vancouver Avenue. The 1900 Portland City Directory also states Georg was employed at Schumacher and Jasmann Furrier Company. (Actually he was a partner.)

Georg Jasmann died of tuberculosis in Portland, Oregon, on 25 August 1901. He was 49 years and 2 months. His funeral was held at the German Methodist Episcopal Church in Portland, Oregon.

According to her death records, Johanna Engel Jasmann died 21 June 1915 of angina pectoris. She was 61 years old. Her funeral was also held at the German Methodist Episcopal Church in Portland, Oregon.

The Jasmann children were:

1. Lydia b 12 November 1878, Bon Homme County, Dakota Territory
2. Johanna Rosine b 9 November 1880, Scotland, Bon Homme County, SD
3. Jennie b November 1881, Scotland, Bon Homme County, SD, m Charles A. Rieha 27 December 1916. Jennie was a candy dipper at a local candy factory; Charles was a machinist
4. George H. b December 1883, m Nan Ross
5. Elizabeth b 29 December 1884, m Julius Rudolph Franzen 28 February 1915

By 1910, **John L. Sayler** owned Jasmann's original tract of land.

Georg Jasmann Sr.
Georg Fredrich Jasmann Sr. was born 27 November 1819 in Worms, South Russia. He was the son of **Johann Georg** and **Eva Fercho Jasmann**. Records for Johann Jassman vary concerning the information about him. First, there are a number of discrepancies about his year of birth. The Rohrbach 1860 death records state Johann Jasmann was born in Sattrach, Prussia, around 1782. He was 80 years when he died on 4 November 1862 in Worms. Karl Stumpp states in the "Worms," section of *The Emigration from Germany to Russia in the Years 1763 to 1862* that Johann was 36, wife Eva was 26, and they had two sons Adolf, 7, and Johann, 1. Stumpp states that they arrived in Worms around 1813 from Poland. Another source, *Worms, Beresan District Odessa, 1858 Census*, states that Johann Jasmann arrived in the colony in 1813 and at the time of the census, he was 78.

The 1830 Rohrbach records indicate Eva Feroch Jasmann died in Worms 20 July 1834. She was 44. The Worms 1858 records show that Johann Jasmann remarried. His second wife's name was **Agatha** and she was 59 years old. Johann Jasmann died 4 November 1862 in Worms. The family was Evangelical Lutheran.

The records indicate Johann and Eva Jasmann had the following children:

1. Adolf Jasmann b 1809 in Poland

2. Johann Jasmann b 1815 in Worms, South Russia m Johanna (Schindler)[1] b ~1822; children Philip d 1852; Jakob b ~1851; Karl b~1854; Katharina b ~1855.[2]
3. Christian Jasmann b 1817 in Worms, South Russia.
4. Phillip Jasmann b 27 November 1819, Worms, South Russia
5. George Fredrick Jasmann b 27 November 1819, Worms, South Russia
6. Paul Jasmann m Christina Serr
7. Elizabetha b 1822 d 7 Sept 1842; records state that she is 20 yrs, 17 days[3]
8. Anna Jasmann m a Polish nobleman___ Von Ischinko. They remained in Europe.
9. Christian b 5 June 1833 in Waterloo m1 Christine Bettger b Rohrbach; m2 Katharina Weikum 14 Nov 1871 Worms; Christian d 23 Nov 1875 in Johannesthal (42 yrs 5 mos 18 dys)[4]

Weidenbach's information includes a parochial record from Worms, Russia, that states the following about Georg Friedrich Jasmann Sr.:

George Friedrich Jassmann, Worms Colonist, Evangelical Lutheran Confession, born the 27 of November, 1819 at Worms. Confirmed in the year 1835. Married on the twelfth of November, 1846 with Elizabeth, born Weidenbach, Evangelical Reformed Confession, born the first of February, 1829.
Their children:
1. Christian b 2 November 1848, Worms, SR.* Confirmed 21 April 1863, m Catherine Vaatz
2. Elizabeth b 13 July 1850, Worms, SR.* Confirmed 28 March, 1865, m Henry Sieler
3. George b July, 1852, Worms, SR.* Confirmed 16 April 1867.

[1] Odessa Digital Library, St. Petersburg Archives, Rohrbach Marriage Records, 183x (D. Wahl). http://pixel.cs.vt.edu/library/stpete/rohr/link/rohr183m.txt.
[2] *1858 Worms Census.*
[3] Odessa Digital Library, St. Petersburg Archives, Rohrbach Death Records, 184x (D. Wahl). http://pixel.cs.vt.edu/library/stpete/rohr/link/rohr184d.txt.
[4] Odessa Digital Library, St. Petersburg Archives, Rohrbach Death Records, 187x (D. Wahl). http://pixel.cs.vt.edu/library/stpete/rohr/link/rohr187d.txt.

4. **Rosine b 29 August 1855, Worms, SR.**
5. **David b 6 June 1857 Worms, SR.* Confirmed 9 April 1872.**

For the second time, married 5 December, 1861 with Magdalena born Mitsel of the Evangelical Reformed Confession.
1. Heinrich b 21 December 1862*

For the third time [George Friedrich Jassman] married: 26 February 1867 born (Catherine) Muller. Their child:
1. Frederick b 24 January 1868

With the exception of these two minor children, all others ad sacra admitted.

This certifies in verbal accord with the church books of the Evangelical Lutheran Church District of Worms, sub-fide pastorial sigillogue ecclesiastice.

Worms, 26 September 1872

*[*denotes those who came to America
and have biographies in this book.]*

Georg's first wife Elizabeth was born in Worms, South Russia, to **Georg Heinrich Weidenbach** and **Anna Margaretta Kussler**. Elizabeth's father, two brothers, and their families also came to Dakota Territory. Elizabeth Weidenbach Jassman died in Worms, Russia, in 1861.

Georg Jasmann married a second time, this time to **Magdalena Mitzel** *(spelling variation Muetsel) **Wagner Hauck**.

Information gathered by Renz shows that Magdalena's first husband was **Lorenz Wagner** from Neu-Danzig. They had three children:

1. Wilhelm b 10 October 1848
2. Ludwig b 8 January 1851 m Juliana Meth of Neu-Danzig
   (They settled in Aberdeen, South Dakota)
3. Dorothea b 16 April 1855

*Magdalena Mitzel Wagner Hauck Jasmann—2nd wife of Georg
Jasmann—and son Michael who also migrated to Dakota Territory
and settled in Scotland, SD in 1886.*

Sometime before 1858, Lorenz Wagner died. Magdalena Mitzel Wagner married for a second time on 13 May 1858 to **Gottfried Hauck** of Rohrbach. On 10 May 1859 their son Michael was born. Gottfried died 15 January 1860 in Johannestal. He was 46 years old. On 5 December 1861, Magdalena married **Georg Friedrich Jasmann**. They had one child, **Heinrich**, born 21 December 1862. Sometime between 1862 and 1867, Magdalena died. Georg Fredrich Jasmann married for a third time on 26 February 1867 to **Catharina Barbara Müller (Mueller) Diede Kussler.**

Catharina Barbara Müller was born circa 1824 to **Jakob Müller** and **Anna Maria Mühleisen.** According to Karl Stumpp's *The Emigration from Germany to Russia in the Years 1763 to 1862*, Jakob was born 1784 and died 30 July 1838 in Johannestal at the age of 53 years and 11 months.[1] Jakob's wife Anna Marie Mühleisen was born circa 1793[2] and, according to *Johannestal Beresan District Odessa 1858 Census*, died in 1856. The family came from Neckartailfingen/Nurtingen-Wuerttemberg in 1817.[3] The revised 1825 census shows that Jakob and Anna Maria Müller had the following children: Anna Margareta 5, Christian 1, and (Catharina) Barbara 1 (apparently Barbara and Christian are twins.)[4] The 1858 census states that Christian Müller also had sisters Rebekka (married **Jacob Mutschelknaus**, see biography*) and Regina (married **Stephan Zimmerman**).

The St. Petersburg files for Rohrbach indicate Catharina Mueller's first marriage on 9 November 1843 was to **Michael Diede** (2). Michael Diede could possibly be the same person who Stumpp lists in the 1825 census for Johannestal. The record states that he is 2, his father Michael (1) 32, mother Anna Christina 31, and siblings Gottlieb 8, and Anna Christina 6. Michael Diede (2) died 1 January 1852 in Johannestal. At the time of his death, he was 28 years and 11 months.

[1] Odessa Digital Library, St. Petersburg Archives, Rohrbach Death Records, 183x (D. Wahl), http://pixel.cs.vt.edi/library/stpete/rohr/link/rohr1830d.txt
[2] Stumpp, p. 714
[3] Ibid.
[4] Ibid.

According to the Rohrbach birth records for the 1840's and 1850's, Catharina Müller and Michael Diede had the following children:

1. Christian b 3 January 1844 Johannestal
2. Gottlieb b 29 January 1845 Johannestal d 12 February 1846
3. Johann Christian b 19 January 1847 Johannestal
4. Jacob b 26 September 1851 in Johannestal

Records reveal Catharina Diede then married **Johannes Kussler** on 11 July 1854 in Rohrbach. The 1850 marriage records indicate that Johannes was a widower and Lutheran (See Kussler biography). After Kussler died, Catharina Müller married **Georg Friedrich Jasmann** on 26 February 1867 in Worms.[1] According to the Rohrbach birth records, she gave birth to Frederich on 24 January 1868. The Jasmann family: Georg 52, Catherina 44, Georg 20, Rosina 18, David 15, Heinrich 9, and Friedrich 4 were part of the third group of German-Russians that departed for America on 13 November 1872 from Hamburg to New York aboard the Hamburg steamer *Silesia*.

After spending the winter at Sandusky, these German-Russian immigrants sent a group of scouts to find enough farmland on which their party could settle. Georg Friedrich Jasmann Sr., his sons Christian and Georg Jr., and Heinrich and Dominic Stoller were the first Germans from South Russia to step on Dakota ground.[2]

Once the party arrived in Dakota Territory, Catherine Jasmann also filed for naturalization, qualifying for homestead land. While she filed on the northwest section of 28, her husband Georg Sr. claimed the northeast and southeast quarters of section 29 and the southwest section of 28. Georg Sr. and Catherine donated a portion of the southwest quarter of section 28 for the sole purpose of building a church.

The WPA South Dakota Graves Registration form states that the church is the "oldest settlement here in Dakota Territory." It was deeded on 29 December 1885 at 12:00 and filed by Georg Jasmann

---

[1] Odessa Digital Library, St. Petersburg Archives, Rohrbach Marriage Records, 186x (D. Wahl). http://pixel.cs.vt.edu/library/stpete/rohr/link/rohr186m.txt.
[2] Rath, p. 68.

Sr. and his wife Katharina Jasmann for $1. The records state: "to the Trustees of the Evangelical Lutheran Zions Gemeinde of Yankton County—never allow this ground to be used for anything else but for church purposes that is, the erection of a church for the use of the above named Gemeinde and for a burial place of them. Containing 10 acres." The following excerpt states this about the church:

> "The first settlers came from Cherson (district in Russia), where there was a close intermingling of various denominations (that is, Lutheran and Reformed). Though there were two different congregations, one pastor would in many cases serve both Lutheran and Reformed congregations. This did not work in America as it resulted in much wrangling and misunderstanding. Many in America wanted to continue this unionism and the first congregation was a union church, served by a former Catholic priest who had become Protestant. Unfortunately the man was known to drink and it was reported that at one time he conducted church intoxicated. He stayed there only eight months and upon his leaving, the congregation had to pay his salary of about $800."

Along with many other neighbors north and south of Odessa Township, Georg Jasmann Sr. experienced a large prairie fire. The 4 April 1889 issue of *The Scotland Citizen* states the following about the fire:

> **Fire Swept Prairies,**
> **Many Farmers Homes Burned Causing Great Loss**
>
> Since Monday afternoon a fever of excitement has prevailed by the disastrous prairie fires that burned out a large number of farmers on that day and Tuesday. On Monday about noon, while the wind was blowing from the northwest fully 50 miles an hour, and everything as dry as a tinder box, fire started in the high prairie grass close to the railroad track near George Snieder's place two miles northeast of Scotland. The high wind swept the fire along with terrific force and every farmer in its track suffered more or less loss. George Jassman Sr. near Odessa church, barn was burned.

Georg Jasmann Sr. died from a stroke on 15 September 1890. *The Scotland Citizen* carried the following about him when he died:

> **George F. Jasmann, died suddenly Monday morning at 3 o'clock from apoplexy. He had had previously two attacks of apoplexy from which he never recovered and this last one his vitality could not resist. Mr. Jasmann was one of the first of the German-Russians colony that emigrated to Dakota nearly twenty years ago, settling with his family at the Odessa church southeast of Scotland. He was a man of means and large influence among his people and his life was one of usefullness and good deeds. He was 70 years and 10 months old, and is survived by his wife. Three of his sons Christian, George and Henry reside in Scotland and David at Portland, Oregon. His remains were burried [sic] in the Scotland cemetery Tuesday afternoon and were attended to their last resting place by a large following of friends.**

Georg F. Jasmann is buried in the Rosehill Cemetery in Scotland. Catharina Jasmann died 11 February 1900 of old age. She is buried in the Odessa Lutheran Cemetery.[1]

By 1910, Georg Jasmann Sr.'s land was owned by the following: **Gottlieb Mutschelknaus**, the southwest quarter of section 28 and the southeast quarter of section 29, and **Wilhelm Mueller**, the northeast quarter of section 29. **Jacob Gimbel** owned Catharine Jasmann's northwest quarter section of 28.

The following sons also immigrated to America with Georg Jasmann Sr. but never homesteaded in Odessa Township, Yankton County:

David Jasmann was born 6 June 1857 in Worms, South Russia to Georg Friedrich Jasmann and **Elizabeth Weidenbach**. He was 15 in December 1872 when he arrived in America aboard the *Silesia*. Although David Jasmann never homesteaded in Odessa Township, he farmed for his father Georg Sr. until he moved to Scotland where he owned and operated a clothing store.

---

[1] Amelia Weidenbach.

The 28 August 1884 issue of *Scotland Dakota Citizen* states:

> **Now is the time to buy Clothing at Dave Jasmann's. He has just received a large stock of Clothing and Furnishing Goods. Try him before you try elsewhere.**

Sometime before 1888, Jasmann sold his business and moved his family to Portland, Oregon.

According to the 1900 *Portland City Directory*, David Jasmann lived at 575 Vancouver Avenue and was working in the wood and coal business. The David Jasmann family then moved to Spokane, Washington, and finally Ritzville, Washington.

David Jasmann married **Mary Hetzler** who was born August 1858 in Missouri. Their children were as follows:

1. Roland b August 1884, d 1918, buried Odessa Cemetery, Odessa, Washington
2. Ida A. b 12 June 1886, d 21 June 1966 King County, Washington, buried Odessa Cemetery, Odessa, Washington

David Jasmann died at his home in Ritzville, Washington, on 8 May 1924 when he was 67 years old. Funeral services were held at the Congregational Church at Odessa, Washington.

Mary Hetzler Jasmann died at a Spokane hospital 9 October 1948 when she was 90. Funeral services were in the care of Smith Funeral Home. She was buried at the Odessa Cemetery, Odessa, Washington.

Fredrich G. Jasmann was born 24 January 1868 in Worms, South Russia, to Georg Friedrich Jasmann and **Catharine Müller**. He married **Rosina Gaier**. Around 1890, the couple and their family moved to Oregon. Jasmann is listed in the *Portland City Directory* of 1890-1891. One entry states that he is a clerk for the India Packing Company. The family is also listed in the 1900 Oregon census as living on Russell Street, Portland City, Multnomah County. Fredrich died when he was 49 on 15 May 1917 in Lincoln County, Washington. He is buried in the Odessa Cemetery in Odessa, Washington.

Listed in a Spokane city directory for 1923, Rosina ("Rosa") was the head of the houshold at West 1634 Riverside Avenue. Her son Herman H. Jasmann lived with her, as well as daughter Gertrude who worked as a stenographer for an insurance company. The 1930 and 1932 city directories for Spokane state that Rosa was living with Herman and Norine Jasmann at South 2412 Jefferson.

Fredrich and Rosina Jasmann's children:

1. Clara b May 1887, Dakota Territory
2. George Edward Jasmann b 9 April 1889 (either died as infant or is same as #3)
3. Edward G. b April 1890, South Dakota
4. Herman H. b September 1891, Oregon, m Norine Mueller, d 15 April 1972 Spokane, Washington
5. Mary b March 1897, Oregon, m Siegmund John Sieler
6. Gertrude b 1899, Oregon

Henry Georg(e) Jasmann, born in Worms, South Russia, on 21 December 1862 was the only son of **Georg Frederich** and **Magdalina (Mitzel Wagner Hauck) Jasmann** (spelling variation Metzel). Henry Georg Jasmann married **Minnie Winkel** of German descent. The family moved to Portland, Oregon before 1890.

The *1900 Portland City Directory* states that Henry George and family resided at 426 Kearney Street and was in the "steam wood saw" business. Before 1904, he and his family moved to 341 Russell where he was listed as a cement contractor.

Henry George Jasmann died in Portland 25 June 1923 at the age of 61. Minnie Winkel Jasmann died in Portland 8 November 1926 at the age of 64.

Their children were:

1. Maximillian b June 1885 in SD
2. Alexander b November 1887 in SD
3. Otto b February (year unknown) in Oregon
4. Ernest b 1892 in Oregon, d 18 June 1953
5. Hugo b September 1897 Oregon
6. Ruth b 5 April 1904

(Georg) Heinrich Jasmann

According to Rohrbach birth files, **Heinrich Jasmann** was born in 8 July 1855 to parents **Phillip** and **Rosina Schindler Jasmann** of Worms, South Russia.[1] But in the Dakota Declaration of Intent, Jasmann listed his birth year as 1851, possibly in order to obtain free land.[2] In fact, the 30 July 1873 ship records for the *Thuringia* state Heinrich was 18 when he came to America with his parents and siblings.

Heinrich Jasmann applied for naturalization along with his father on 9 August 1873 and received naturalization papers in 1878. His land consisted of the northeast quarter of section 7 and the southwest quarter of section 8. By 1910 Heinrich Sayler owned the southwest quarter of section 8 and Frank Cherney owned the northeast quarter of section 7.

Heinrich's first wife was cousin **Rosina Jasmann**, daughter of **Georg Fredrich Jasmann Sr.** and his first wife, **Elizabeth Weidenbach**. Rosina was born 29 August 1855 in Worms. The *Scotland Journal* 28 August 1890 states the following about Rosina Jasmann:

> **Mrs. Henry Jassman died early Monday morning from the effects of a fall from a chair Saturday that caused a premature birth. The funeral occured [sic] from the Luthren [sic] church Tuesday afternoon Rev. August Miller officiating, and the large number in attendance testified to the esteem which the deceased was held by her acquaintances. A husband and six children, the eldest 11 years old, are left to mourn her sad and untimely death. They have the sincere sympathy of all in their affliction.**

---

[1] Odessa Digital Library, St. Petersburg Archives, Rohrbach Birth Records, 185x (D. Wahl). http://pixel.cs.vt.edu/library/stpete/rohr/link/rohr185b.txt.

[2] Odessa Digital Library, Dakota Declarations of Intent (A. Brosz). http://pixel.cs.vt.edu/library/odessa.html.

Heinrich and Rosina's children:

1. Julia b 19 March 1879, Dakota Territory, bap 25 March 1879 by Pastor Beckmann, m Christ Kuch
2. Heinrich George b 24 November 1880, Dakota Territory, bap 19 December 1880 by Pastor Bischoff
3. Pauline b January 1883, Oregon, m John Schoppert
4. William b October 1884, Dakota Territory
5. Waldamor Theodor b 28 July 1886, Dakota Territory, bap 20 November 1886 by Pastor Miller
6. Herbert Albert b 5 September 1888, Dakota Territory, bap 10 November 1889 by Pastor Miller

Heinrich Jasmann married a second time. The 1900 Oregon census states that the Jasmanns lived in Englewood Precinct, Marion County. In addition to the known information about Heinrich, his second wife, **Minnie**, was born in November 1863 in Germany. Children of this union who were still living at home at the time were Rudolf, born March 1898 in Oregon; Otto, born November 1899 in Oregon; William, born October 1894 in Dakota; Walter, born July 1886 in Dakota; and Herbert, born September 1888 in Dakota.

Phillip Jasmann
    Phillip Jasmann was born on 27 November 1819 at Worms, South Russia. The son of **Johann** and **Eva Jasmann**, Phillip is assumed to have been the twin of Georg Friedrich Jasmann of sections 28 and 29.
    Phillip married **Rosina Schindler** 6 June 1854 in Worms.[1] The Rohrbach marriage files state that the couple was Lutheran. They and their children, Heinrich 18, Wilhelm 14, Phillip 12, Anton 9, Friedrich 5, and Henrietta 16, embarked from Hamburg, Germany, on the steamship *Thuringia*, arriving in New York 30 July 1873.[2]
    An article from *The Chicago Tribune*, dated 4 August 1873, states the following about Phillip Jasmann:

---

[1] Odessa Digital Library, St. Petersburg Archives, Rohrbach Marriage Records, 185x (D. Wahl). http://pixel.cs.vt.edu/library/stpete/rohr/link/rohr185m.txt.

[2] *Heritage Review*, June 1973, p. 47.

A party of about 100 left the old country and settled near Yankton, Dakota Territory, and they were so well satisfied with our laws and the productiveness of the soil, that they were soon followed by 500 more. These parties are very wealthy, and are said to be worth over two millions of dollars in the aggregate. The richest, as well as the most intelligent, in the party, is Mr. Philip Jassmann, who has with him about $100,000 in cash, many others are worth from $500 to $10,000. This acquisition to the population of Dakota will be of immense benefit to that Territory.

Phillip applied for and received his naturalization papers in 1880. His land was the southeast quarter of section 7 and the northwest quarter of section 17.

The following list is taken from the Rohrbach birth and death records for the 1850's-70's, identifying Phillip and Rosina's children:

1. (Georg) Heinrich* b 8 July 1855, Worms, m Rosina Jasmann* (b 29 August 1855)
2. (Henrika) Henrietta b 21 May 1857, Worms, d 14 February 1941 Portland, Oregon, m Daniel Frey (d 6 October 1935), buried Riverview Cemetery, Portland, Oregon
3. Wilhelm* b 26 Jan 1859, Worms
4. Phillip Jr. b 18 March 1861
5. Anton b 1 April 1863
6. Pauline 3 Feb 1868 d 20 April 1869
7. Friedrich b April 1 Feb 1870, Worms, d 29 December 1957 Alameda, California, wife 1 Lillie b August 1876, wife 2 Doris

Phillip Jasmann's farm was damaged heavily in the 4 April 1889 prairie fire. The *Scotland Citizen* states: "The large frame house of Phillip Jassman's farm, occupied by M. Schook, together with barns and machinery were burned. Loss $3000."

Ken Gulling's research on the Jasmann family shows that Phillip and Rosina moved to Oregon. Phillip died 13 July 1897 in Grants Pass. After Phillip died, Rosina went to live with her daughter and her other children. The 1900 Oregon census has "Jasman, Rosa b

8/34 Russia, living in Tangent, Linn County with her son [son-in-law] Daniel Frey, husband of daughter Henrietta."
Rosina Jasmann died 6 February 1927 at the age of 92 years. She was buried at the Rose City Cemetery, Portland, Oregon.

Wilhelm Jasmann

Wilhelm Jasmann was born to **Phillip** and **Rosina Jasmann** on 26 January 1859 in Russia. He was 14 when he came to America with his parents and siblings in 1873. He applied for naturalization and received it in 1881. Wilhelm Jasmann's homestead land was the northeast quarter of section 18 and the northwest quarter of section 20. Gulling's research also shows that Wilhelm Jasmann died 27 February 1884.

By 1910 **Christian** and **Anton Libakken** shared ownership in Jasmann's original claim to the northeast quarter of section 18 and **Heinrich Auch** owned the northwest quarter of section 20.

Kost
David Kost

David Kost, born 28 April 1853, was the son of **Jacob** and **Margaretha Lutz Kost**. He arrived in New York aboard the *Frisia* on 16 July 1873 along with his parents, brothers, and sister. Born circa 1853, he and wife **Louisa** had homestead land on the southwest quarter of section 22.

(Johann) Jakob Kost

Jacob Kost married **Margaretha Lutz** 5 October 1840 in Rohrbach. Pastor Bonekemper officiated at the marriage.[1] Jacob's parents are presumed to be **David** and **Katharina Mulbeyer (Muehlbeier)**. Katharina died in Worms 6 April 1854 at the age of 54 years, 3 months. She was Lutheran.

Jacob was 57, his wife **Margaretha Lutz Kost** 52, and their children David 20, Jakob 12, Frederick 9, Carl 5, and Christine 2 left Russia and arrived in New York aboard the steamer *Frisia* on

---

[1] Odessa Digital Library, St. Petersburg Archives, Rohrbach Marriage Records, 184x, (D. Wahl). http://pixel.cs.vt.edu/library/stpete/rohr/link/rohr184m.txt.

16 July 1873.[1]

The Yankton County, Dakota Territory, 1880 U.S. Federal Census states that Jacob was born in Russia and his parents were both born in Wuerttemburg, Germany. Jacob's father was.David Kost who was born in 1788.[2] Margaretha Lutz was born in Russia and both of her parents were born in Germany.

Jacob Kost homesteaded the southeast quarter of section 22. Margaretha Lutz Kost died at Wolf Creek, Hutchinson County, South Dakota, 29 May 1908 at the age of 85 years 5 months and 12 days.

Jacob and Margaretha Kost's children:

1. Anna Maria b Oct 1841, Balditzki, SR
2. Catharina b June 1848, Balditzki, SR
3. Peter b 30 June 1846 Balditzki, SR d 24 Feb 1846
4. David b 28 April 1853, Worms
5. Christian b 17 Aug 1856, Worms, d 17 Jan 1858
6. Jacob (is not listed in the Rohrbach records)
7. Philipp b 5 May 1862, Worms
8. Karl b 24 May 1867 Worms

Kussler, Kusler
Jacob Kussler

Jacob Kussler was born 11 August 1838 in Worms, South Russia, to **Johannes** and **Elizabeth Munsch** (sp variation) **Kussler**. A researcher for the Kusler family, Della Kiesz, claims the Kussler family originally immigrated to Russia from an area west of the Rhine River, Bavaria, Germany. This area would eventually become part of Pfalz. Elizabeth Munsch died 17 January 1854 in Worms. The records state that she was 37 years and 6 months when she died. She was also Lutheran. Johannes and Elizabeth Kussler had the following children according to the St. Petersburg birth and death files for Rohrbach:

1. Elisabeth b 22 August 1833 Worms Bap: Aug 23 d 20 March 1835 1 year old

---

[1] *Heritage Review*, June 1973, p. 39.
[2] Della Kiesz, genealogical research.

STEPPES TO NEU ODESSA 59

2. Louisa? b 1 July 1835 Worms Bapt 2-July d 18 July 1835 17 days old
3. Margaretha 1 July 1835 Worms Bapt 2-July d 8 July 1835 7 days old
4. Catharina b 3 August 1836 Worms Bapt 9-Aug
5. Jacob b 11 August 1838 Worms
6. Georg b 9 September 1840 in Worms
7. Johann d 16 Oct 1846 3 yrs old at the time of death
8. Elisabeth b 20 March 1845 in Worms
9. Johannes b 6 November 1846 in Worms*
10. Heinrich b 14 September 1848 Worms
11. Adam b April 1852 Worms
12. Margaretha b April 1852 Worms d 4 February 1853 Worms 9 m

After Elizabeth's death, records indicate that **Johannes Kussler** married **Catharina Müller Diede** 11 July 1854 in Rohrbach. The 1850 marriage records indicate that Johannes was a widower and Lutheran.[1]

According to the 1850 birth records, Johann Kussler and Catharina Müller of Worms had a son named Heinrich born 20 June 1855. The child was baptized 10 July 1855 in the Reformed Church. The 1850 Rohrbach death records for Worms show on 1 February 1856, Heinrich Kussler, a 9-month child of Johannes Kussler, died. The *Worms Beresan District Odessa 1858 Census* shows that the Kusslers also had a daughter Regina* who was 1.

Johann Kussler's death is not listed in the St. Petersburg files, but **Catharina Muller Diede Kussler** married **Georg Jasmann** on 26 February 1867.*

Jacob Kussler married **(Eva) Catharina Schaefer** who was born 10 June 1838. Catharina's parents were **Valentine** and **Anna Maria Schatz Schaefer** of Johannestal.*[2]

Jacob, Catharina, and their children were part of a third group that left Russia in the late fall of 1872 and came to America on the steamship *Tiger*. They landed in New York on 2 December 1872

[1] Odessa Digital Library, St. Petersburg Archives, Rorhbach Marriage Records, 185x, (D Wahl). http://pixel.cs.vt.edu/library/stpete/rohr/link/rohr185m.txt.

[2] Odessa Digital Library, St. Petersburg Archives, Rorhbach Birth Records, 183x, (D Wahl). http://pixel.cs.vt.edu/library/stpete/rohr/link/rohr183b.txt.

then arrived by train at Sandusky, Ohio, sometime before the 15th of December 1872. Once in Sandusky, they stayed the winter with others who had also immigrated to America from Russia.

Friedrich Mutschelknaus, who also homesteaded in Odessa Township and was "an eyewitness on the journey of the second group," stated the following:

"**From Worms** there were Jakob and Johann Kussler and others. The second group was still occupied with the harvest, threshing and selling or auctioning its wheat. (The first group had sold its wheat on the stalk.)

On October 17, 1872 the second group left Johannestal to take the train in Odessa. On the evening of October 17, 1872 we came to Odessa and in the morning of the next day at 7 o'clock we took the train for Germany. After three days we arrived at Hamburg, where we stayed for two days. A steamship brought us from Hamburg to Hull on the east coast of England. The North Sea was at that time quite turbulent and right then we became acquainted with sea sickness. With the railroad we went from Hull to Liverpool.

On Saturday evening about 7 o'clock we came to Liverpool and had to wait for four days till [sic] we were brought to the big ocean-going vessel. So far everything went rather well. But when we had traveled westward for three days and three nights, we ran into a violent storm. The doors were tightly closed so that nobody could get out. The high waves dashed over the ship that was severely damaged. The cabin was destroyed, on the deck many things were swept away and finally the ship's screw was so badly damaged that it could not be used any more.

It happened with us that bad night as with the people of Israel in the wilderness and we cried: 'Were there no graves for us in Russia that we have to drown here?' But where danger is greatest, God's help is nearest. Nobody drowned, the storm subsided. Since the ship was too damaged, they could not go any farther and had to turn around yet the same night and when we got on deck again the next morning, we noticed that we were going eastward instead of westward. The engine could not be used any more and the ship had set sail. For

> coming back to Ireland we needed this time six days and six nights.
> In the Irish port we had to wait three days till [sic] another ship came. Then it took us three days again until all the goods were transferred to that ship; and only on the fourth day were we ready to depart for the west. Since we now had a smooth, high running sea we were on the water altogether thirty-six days." [1]

The Kusslers spent the winter in Sandusky with others who had emigrated from Russia. In the spring, after the scouts found land in Yankton County, Dakota Territory, for their whole group to homestead, they moved to Odessa Township and settled on the northern half of section 31. In 1873 Jacob Kussler also bought 160 acres of land in Bon Homme County, section 2 of Township 95, Range 58, from Vallentin Schaeffer. This land was situated next to Ludwig Kussler's (of the same township, range, and section). In 1880 Jacob received his naturalization papers.

Although no church record states whether Jacob and family were of either the Reformed or the Lutheran faith, the WPA cemetery records for the German Reformed Odessa Church states that the location of the church and cemetery was on the southwest quarter of the northeast quarter of section 31, Township 96 N of Range 57 W, in the county of Yankton. This land had previously been where Jacob Kussler had homesteaded.

Jacob Kussler owned and operated a general merchandise store in Scotland. The various editions of *The Scotland Citizen* mention Kusler and his family.

> 25 November 1888 - Jacob Kusler will move to Eureka next spring with his stock of general merchandise.
>
> 13 December 1888 - Jacob Kusler packed and shipped his stock of general merchandise to his new location at Eureka this week. Henry Kusler, his son, moved his family at the same time and will open out the new store. Mrs. Kusler will remain in Scotland until spring to close up his outstanding amounts.

---

[1] Rath, pp. 61-62.

---

25 April 1889 - Jacob Kusler moved his family to Eureka on Tuesday.

According to the 1880 U.S. Federal Census, the following children were living with Jacob and Catharina:

1. Heinrich b 1861
2. Sophia b 1863
3. Katharina b 1865
4. Johann b 1869
5. Christina b 1875
6. Jacob b 1878[1]

Sometime before 1905, and after Katherina Schaeffer had died, Jacob returned to Scotland, S.D., and married **Rosina Schaeffer Auch**, the widow of **Jacob Auch** who also settled in the Odessa Township.

Johann Kussler

Johann Kussler was born 6 November 1846 in Worms, South Russia. His father was Johann Kussler Sr. His mother was Elizabetha Munsch. The Kussler family originally arrived in Russia from an area west of the Rhine River in what was once part of Bavaria, Germany.[2]

In 1866 Johann married **Christina Schaeffer**, who was born 15 June 1847. She was the daughter of **Vallentin** and **Anna Maria Schaeffer**.[3]*

In 1872 the Kussler family was part of the second group to leave Russia. After leaving Johannestal, South Russia, the Kusslers arrived in Hamburg, Germany. They boarded the *Leopard* and "'[d]uring the first days of December we landed happily in New York.'"[4] They wintered in Sandusky and joined two other groups of German-Russians traveling to Odessa Township, Yankton County, Dakota Territory, in the spring of 1873.

---

[1] Kusler, p. 12.
[2] Ibid. p. 13.
[3] Ibid.
[4] Rath, p. 62.

Johann Kusler, 1846-1921.
Photo courtesy of Walter M. Kusler.

Johann Kussler applied for naturalization and received it in 1880. He homesteaded on the southern half of section 30 where "[o]n October 15, 1880, for the sum of $4.00 [Johann] made the balance of payment on 160 acres in Yankton County, the SE 1/4 Section of 30-96-57."[1]

Johann was one of the original founders of the German Reformed Odessa Church. After the turn of the century, the family moved to North Dakota.

> *Johann, or John Sr. as sometimes referred to, lived with his family in South Dakota for 29 years and in June of 1902 all of his family moved to Logan County on a farm 2 ½ miles south of Fredonia, ND. After that he retired to Kulm for 11 [years], and moved into Fredonia in 1913. His burial place is a little ways north of Fredonia, ND.*[2]

Deborah Lee Rothery's research states that Johann Kussler died 23 Dec 1921. Christina died in Fredonia, North Dakota, on 2 September 1928. She was 81. Rothery also lists their children (*note: this family has dropped an 's' from their name*):

1. Jacob Kusler b 1868, d 1887

---

[1] Kusler, p. 13.
[2] Ibid. p. 14.

2. Elisabeth Kusler b 20 July 1870, SR, d 10 April 1938, Fredonia, ND, m 1903 William Orth (b 24 December 1867, d 1947)
3. John Kusler, Jr. b 28 October 1871, Worms, SR, d 24 June 1957, Kulm, ND, m Scotland, SD, 2 January 1894 Magdalena Grosz (b 24 July 1872, Kulm, Bessarabia, SR, d 15 June 1956 Morton, WA). Magdalena came to America with her parents in 1875 and settled in Scotland, DT. Parents: Daniel Grosz b 8 September 1846, Kulm, Bessarabia, SR, d 14 January 1919 Parkston, SD, and Justina Dietrich b 7 August 1849 Paris, Bessarabia, SR, d 28 November 1929 Parkston, SD. John Kusler first homesteaded at Lynch, Nebraska. They moved 11 miles southwest of Kulm, ND. John retired in 1925 from farming and moved into Kulm.
4. Henry Kusler b 2 January 1874, Yankton County, DT, d Fredonia, ND, 3 October 1932, m 2 February 1900 Elizabeth Schemp (b 7 Sept 1875, d 30 July 1929).
5. Adam Kusler b 25 October 1876, Yankton, DT, d 21 March 1899, Kulm, ND, m Regina Serr (b 3 October 1873, d 8 August 1964).
6. Gottlieb Kusler b 2 March 1879 Yankton, DT, m 1904 Katherine Bender (b 20 February 1883, d 24 November 1955). Gottlieb d 1961 Omak, WA.
7. August Kusler b 1 August 1883, Lesterville, DT, d 2 November 1975 Jamestown, ND, m Christine Welfea 3 February 1906.
8. William Kusler a twin.
9. Martha Kusler a twin.

Ludwig Kussler

Ludwig Kussler was born 12 April 1849, the assumed son of **Johann Kussler** and **Elizabeth Munsch** of Worms, South Russia, and brother to **Jacob** and **Johann Kussler** who also immigrated to America.[1]

Ludwig Kussler married **Christiana Schaefer** 2 March 1871. Their marriage is listed in both the Freudental and Rohrbach

---

[1] Kusler, pp. 11-12.

marriage files.[1] The records show that Christiana Schaefer was born 9 April 1853 to **Heinrich** and **Rosina Gottlieba Hartlaub Schaefer**.[2]

Ludwig, Christiana, and their nine-month-old child Elizabeth were part of the second group that immigrated to America from Russia in the late fall of 1872.[3] After wintering in Sandusky, Ohio, they also joined the vanguard of immigrants to Dakota Territory. Ludwig homesteaded on the southeast quarter of section 17 in Odessa Township. He received his naturalization records in 1882.

According to the WPA cemetery records, Ludwig Kussler was one of the original founders of the German Reformed Odessa Church located on section 31.

Ludwig and Christiana's children were:

1. Elizabeth b 27 February 1872, Rohrbach, SR, d 3 June 1949, Tripp, SD, m1 August Tislau, m2 5 February 1895 George Bitterman (b 31 January 1869, d 3 August 1948)
2. John L. b 5 June 1875, Scotland, DT, d 24 September 1964, Scotland, SD, m Carolina Ulmer (b 7 September 1876, d 16 April 1962, Scotland, SD)
3. Henry b 14 May 1879, Scotland, DT, d 9 February 1959, Hazen, ND, m 14 January 1902 Magdalena Schmoll
4. Regina b 8 July 1877, Scotland, DT, d January 1952, m Philip Preszler
5. Emma b 30 October 1885, Scotland, DT, d 7 November 1975, Los Angeles, CA, m Theodore Engle (b 7 July 1883, Mound City, DT, d 6 June 1960, Cathay, ND)
6. Emanuel b 31 October 1883, Scotland, DT, d 2 March 1972, Beulah, ND, m1 1905 Louisa Schrink (b 3 June 1882, d 11 December 1917), m2 26 Febuary 1918 Ida Fischer (b 1 Aug 1898, d 23 January 1977)

---

[1] Odessa Digital Library, St. Petersburg Archives, Rohrbach Marriage Records, 187x (D. Wahl). http://pixel.cs.vt.edu/library/stpete/rohr/link/rohr187m.txt., and Freudental Marriage Records, 187x (R. Wiseman). http://pixel.cs.vt.edu/library/stpete/freud/link/freu187m.txt.

[2] Odessa Digital Library, St. Petersburg Archives, Rohrbach Birth Records, 185x, (D. Wahl). http://pixel.cs.vt.edu/library/stpete/rohr/link/rohr185b.txt.

[3] Rath, p. 63.

Ludwig Kussler died in Delmont, South Dakota, in 1890. Christina Schaefer Kussler then married Michael Kautz who had been divorced.

Michael and Christina had one child:

1. Martha b 15 June 1891, Delmont, SD, d 20 October 1965, Delmont, SD, m John Beck[1]

Mueller
W. Wilhelm Mueller

Wilhelm Mueller was born in Kalmukara (sp. variation: Kalmakara, Kalmuchara), Crimea, Russia, on 15 January 1855 to **Georg Mueller** and **Johanna Guent(h)ner Mueller**.[2]

Georg Mueller Jr.'s father, **Georg Mueller Sr.**, was born near Worms, Germany, in 1786. In 1805 he migrated to Friedental, Crimea, Russia. He married **Rosina Frasch**.

Georg Mueller Jr. and Johanna Guenthner Mueller had thirteen children; not all of them came to America. The following is a list of known children:

1. Friederika Mueller b 11 Oct 1842, Friedental,[3] m Martin Schamber 9 Feb 1860 (Schamber was a school teacher; they lived in Scotland, DT, then moved to ND),[4] d 1893 of nerve fever in North Dakota
2. Karolina Mueller b 12 March 1848 (records show 28 Feb 1848), Kalmakara, Crimea, SR, d 13 March 1939 Menno, SD, m 23 Nov 1865 Friederich Frasch (b 4 January 1845),[5] in Neusatz Parish;[6] Friederich d 7 December 1918.

---

[1] Kusler, pp. 115-120.

[2] Odessa Digital Library, St. Petersburg Archives, Neusatz Birth Records, 185x (G. Bechthold). http://pixel.cs.vt.edu/library/stpete/neusatz/link/neus185b.txt.

[3] Odessa Digital Library, St. Petersburg Archives, Neusatz Birth Records, 184x (G. Bechthold). http://pixel.cs.vt.edu/library/stpete/neusatz/link/neus184b.txt.

[4] See notes on Martin Schamber in Wagner's *Daughters of Dakota*, Appendix A.

[5] *MENNO*, p. 432.

[6] Odessa Digital Library, St. Petersburg Archives, Neusatz Birth Records, 186x (G. Bechthold). http://pixel.cs.vt.edu/library/stpete/neusatz/link/neus186m.txt.

W. Wilhelm Mueller, Fredericka Engel Mueller and family.

The First Reformed Church in Dakota Territory section 31.

3. Jacobine b 16 March 1850 Kalmakara[1]
4. Wilhelm Mueller b 15 January 1855, Kalmakara, SR, d 6
   March 1933, buried Hoffnung Cemetery, m Friedericka
   Engel, dau/o Johann and Elizabeth Engel*
5. Michael Friedrich b 16 Oct. 1856 Friedental, Crimea, SR.
6. Johanna b 31 July 1858 Friedental
7. Dorthea Mueller b 16 December 1859, Kalmakara, SR,[2] d 12
   November 1926, m Henry Haar (b 15 October 1858, d 12
   November 1926). Henry had a farm near Freeman. His
   parents were Christian Haar and Katherine Frasch

W. Wilhelm Mueller left Russia in 1874 when he was 19. He and
friend Peter Zeeb boarded the ship *Lessing* on 24 July 1874 in
Hamburg, Germany. After arriving in New York City, they
continued on to Scotland, Bon Homme County, Dakota Territory.

Wilhelm Mueller applied for his intent to naturalize papers in
Yankton, Dakota Territory, on 17 August 1874.
The German Reformed Odessa Church records state that in 1877,
Wilhelm married Friedericka Engel who was the daughter of
Johann and Elizabeth Berndt Engel. Friedericka was born 15
December 1856 in Alt-Danzig, Russia. She came to America with
her parents aboard the *Westphalia* and arrived in New York from
Hamburg, Germany, on 30 July 1873.
In 1893 the Mueller family joined the German Reformed Odessa
Church. Later they joined the Hoffnung Reformed Church.
Wilhelm homesteaded on the northern half of the northeast
quarter of section 2, the northern half of the northwestern quarter of
section 3 in Odessa Township, and the southeast quarter of section
34 in Sweet Township in Hutchinson County. Later he bought land
east of the Hoffnung Reformed Cemetery that had been originally
zoned for a school. He also bought land from his brother-in-law
Michael Serr. (Michael Serr was married to Katharina Engel, the
sister of Wilhelm's wife Friedericka.) By 1910 Wilhelm Mueller
owned the southwest quarter of section 26, the southeast quarter of

[1] Odessa Digital Library, St. Petersburg Archives, Neusatz Birth Records, 185x (G.
Bechthold). http://pixel.cs.vt.edu/library/stpete/neusatz/link/neus185b.txt.
[2] Ibid.

section 27, the northeast quarter of section 34, the northeast quarter of section 29, and the east half of section 35 in Odessa Township. Wilhelm Mueller acquired enough land before he died to give each of his sons a farm. By 1910 **Peter Schamber** owned the original Mueller homestead land.

The *Scotland Journal* 18 January 1896 states this about Mueller:

> **Wm. Muller a prominent farmer and stockman of Choteau Creek was in the city Wednesday on his way home from Chicago, where he had been with a shipment of stock. He says he struck a good market and is only sorry he didn't have more stock.**

Another article in the 15 February 1896 issue of the *Scotland Journal* states the following about Friedricka and Wilhelm's daughter Sarah:

> **Miss Sarah Miller, aged, 17, died at the home of Jacob Ulrich, in Tyndall on Monday last, after a lingering illness. Her parents reside between Scotland and Lesterville and the young girl had been brought here for treatment. Her case was hopeless when she arrived.** *–Tyndall Register*

Records in the Bon Homme County Court House located in Tyndall, South Dakota, state that Friedericka Engel died on 21 August 1920 of nephritis. Wilhelm Mueller died on 16 March 1933. He is buried in the Hoffnung Reformed Cemetery.

Wilhelm and Friedericka's children:

1. Sarah b 13 October 1878, bap 8 December 1878, d 2 February 1896
2. George b 22 October 1880, bap 1 January 1881, m Regina Schatz 28 February 1905, d 23 November 1922, buried Hoffnung Reformed Cemetery
3. Phillip b 7 May, bap 30 June 1882, m Rose Hauck 6 March 1906, d 10 December 1943, buried Menno, SD

4. Albert b 1 December 1884, bap 30 March 1885, m Paulina Helena Bierle 20 September 1910, d 30 June 1951, buried Rosehill Cemetery, Scotland, SD
5. Gustav(e) b 30 September 1887, bap 1 April 1888, m Martha Louisa Walz 6 October 1920, d 6 October 1960
6. Herbert b 22 December 1892, bap 17 June 1893

Mund, Muend, Mind, Mindt

Georg Mund

Although the way the family spells its name varies, **Georg Mund** was probably born 24 November 1846 in Worms[1] to **Peter Mund** and **Margareth Kost** who married 16 December 1845.[2] He and his family were part of the third group of Germans to leave Russia. On 13 November 1872, Georg 27, Catherina 24, George 4, Jacob 2, and Adam 1/2 boarded the *Silesia* and sailed to America.

Mund homesteaded on the northwest quarter of section 22.

By the 1880 census, Adam and Jacob are not included in the family listing, but the following are:

1. George 12
2. Katie 4
3. Heinrich 2
4. Elizabeth 2/12 - March

The census also states that George Mund was a farmer, that he was born in Russia, and that his parents were born in Russia.

The same census states that Catherina was born in Russia and both parents were also born in Russia.

By the 1910 census Mund's land was owned by **Jacob Stocker**.

---

[1] Odessa Digital Library, St. Petersburg Archives, Rohrbach Birth Records, 184x (D. Wahl). http://pixel.cs.vt.edu/library/stpete/rohr/link/rohr184b.txt.

[2] Odessa Digital Library, St. Petersburg Archives, Rohrbach Marriage Records, 184x (D. Wahl). http://pixel.cs.vt.edu/library/stpete/rohr/link/rohr184m.txt.

Mutschelknaus
Friedrich Mutschelknaus

Friedrich Mutschelknaus was born in Johannestal, South Russia, 26 February 1852 to **Jakob** and **Rebecca Mueller Mutschelknaus***. He was part of the second group of German Russians to arrive in America in 1872. Mutschelknaus reported to the *Dakota Freie Presse* about the group's departure, voyage, and arrival in America:

> To the second part belonged my father Jakob Mutschelknaus, Gottlieb and Ludwig Sailer, sons of old Johannes Sailer, Gottfried Mehrer and others whose names I cannot recall. This second party, leaving, reaped their crops, threshed and sold them, and sold or auctioned off their belongings.
>
> On the 17th of October 1872, the second party left Johannestal to board the train to Odessa. It was a beautiful, sunny autumn day; only our hearts were sad. Especially for me, Friedrich Mutschelknaus, and for my parents-in-law, Gottlieb Delzer. On the 3rd of October of that year, I had been married, and now we were making the long trip to America. My parents-in-law had only one thought, that they would never again see their daughter Caroline.
>
> Among the other families, too, there was much sorrow; for America at that time was a much greater distance from Russia than it is today. "She is leaving and I'll never see her again!" So said my father-in-law. But he was wrong for in September, 1874, my parents-in-law also came to America.
>
> On the evening of the 18th of October, we arrived in Odessa, and on the following morning at about 7:00, we boarded the train for Germany. It took about three days until we arrived at Hamburg where we stopped off for two days. Next a steamboat took us to Hull on the east coast of England. The North Sea was very lively, giving us our first experience with seasickness. From Hull we went to Liverpool by train.

On a Saturday evening at about 7:00, we arrived in Liverpool where we had to wait four days until we were driven to a large ocean liner. Up to now the trip had been tolerable. But after we had steamed three days and three nights toward the west, we encountered terrible storms. Doors were fastened securely so that no one could get out on deck. High waves swept over the ship, damaging it extensively. Much of the superstructure was torn from the deck, and finally the propeller was so damaged that it could no longer be used.

It was for us during that awful night as it was for the tribe of Israel in the Wilderness, and all our people cried out in the anguish and fright, "There were no graves for us in Russia; we had come here to drown." But where one's misery is the greatest, there God's help is the nearest. No one drowned and the storm calmed itself. Because the ship was damaged too extensively, it could no longer proceed and must, therefore, turn around even though at night. When we came on deck in the morning, we saw that instead of proceeding toward the west, we were going toward the east. Because the machines could not be used, the ship had to set sails. The return to Ireland required six days and nights.

We had to wait three days in the Irish port until another ship arrived. Then there was another delay of three days to transfer the stores of the ship, and on the fourth day we were again ready to sail toward the west. Because we again encountered high seas throughout the onward voyage, we were a total of thirty-six days on the water.

Early in December we arrived safely in New York. On account of the shipwreck, we had lost so much time that a third party leaving from Johannestal had passed us and was already on the way to Sandusky, Ohio, by the time we arrived in New York. In the third party were my uncle George Jasman, George's son Christian Jasman, Henry Sieler, Dominic Stoller and others.

"Where do you wish to go?" we were asked in New York. But we were strangers in this country and did not know ourselves. We were told that others of our people had preceded us and had gone to Sandusky, Ohio, so we decided, too, to go to Sandusky. We arrived in Sandusky some time between the 10th and 15th of December, 1872. This was a large manufacturing city, so we found enough empty lodgings to accommodate us.

Because no report of us had been received, those at home in Johannestal thought nothing else than we had drowned in the ocean. As soon as we arrived in Sandusky, I wrote a letter to parents-in-law. This letter was the first evidence of our safe arrival which those in our homeland received, and interest in it was so great that Pastor Birnbach read the letter from the pulpit so that all Johannestal would know of our safe arrival.

By the beginning of March, it was resolved to choose scouts and send them to the West in order to determine where to settle. Among the scouts chosen were George Jasmann, Christian Jasmann, Henry Sieler, Gottfried Mehrer, Jakob Mutschelknaus and Gottlieb Sailer. There were twelve men in all. The Reformed Church minister in Sandusky, Ohio, Pastor Schaf, to whom we always went to church, drew up the route for the scouts. He also sent letters in advance to pastors and members of his church so that when the Sandusky scouts arrived, they could assist them by taking them in and showing them salable land.

The scouts first went to Michigan, Illinois and Wisconsin. They found there that one could buy eighty acres of land here and several miles away additional acres. "No, this isn't what we want" they said, "we want to all be together so that we can have our own church and school." Then was said to them, "Well, people, if that is what you want, then you must go far west of here, as far west as Nebraska." Because it would be too expensive for twelve men to make the trip, it was decided to send six men back to Sandusky, and the remaining six then set out on the trip to Nebraska. Those making the trip west were George Jasmann, Christian Jasmann, Henry Sieler, Dominic Stoller, Jakob Mutschelknaus and Gottlieb Sailer.

...they were advised to go to Dakota to the city of Yankton; there, very likely, they would find land to their liking. Because as previously mentioned, these trips cost so much money, they decided again to separate two from the remaining six scouts, and four men went to Dakota. By this arrangement, Jakob Mutschelknaus and Gottlieb Sailer returned to Sandusky.

The other four went to Dakota where they found land as it had been described to them. Around Yankton and along the Jim (James) River, the land was somewhat settled, but farther out there was nothing but the sky and the land. After they had traveled around, looked at the land and acquainted themselves with the law for taking land, they returned to Sandusky.

It may have been the 25th or the 26th of March, 1873, when the four scouts returned to Sandusky. An afternoon assembly was called in which all Russian Germans took part. The four men reported about the land and how the law for homesteading had been explained to them. They related that they had already seen green crops, and that a farmer near Yankton had told them that the crop was sowed at the end of February. This was almost like it had been for us in Russia.

The scouts declared, "We are firmly resolved that we all go to Dakota Territory, to the city of Yankton. If you have faith in us, then let us go." To that others replied, "If it is good enough for you, then it is good enough for us."

...because we always attended church services there with the German people, we had become well acquainted. When they heard that we had decided to go to Dakota Territory, we were very much pitied by them.

"Oh," they said. "what will you people do there in the wilderness? You won't be able to make a living there. Buffalo and bears and wolves and other animals wander around out there!" The four scouts replied, "We went out on the prairie and saw nothing of all those animals. We shall go." But just to be sure, however, every family provided

> itself with weapons to defend their lives from the buffalo an [sic] bears.[1]

Mutschelknaus goes on to explain that after loading up their belongings, the group boarded the train for a journey that would take them about three days. They were quite surprised when they arrived in Yankton because deep snow covered the ground. Peter Moos from Rohrbach complained and accused the scouts of lying about the Dakota fields being sowed in February. He threatened to go back, but he stayed, "and when the snow melted away, the green crops did appear."

> Several families purchased horses and wagons in order to drive out into the country to look for a place to settle. The old surveyor Maier always went along on these drives. Generally in the morning after breakfast, we would take off across the prairie. We would take our noon meal along, but by night we would have to be back in Yankton; for out there away from the city, there was nothing but the barren prairie.

> ...One claim after another was surveyed, going four miles north, then turning about and surveying the claims going south. So it went, up and down, toward the west until claims had been surveyed for everyone. I believe it took us two days to do all the surveying. This colony received the name "Odessa Settlement" because all of our people had lived in the Odessa District in the old country.
> And so it was. With industry and thrift and with God's blessing on the work of our hands the most of us have become well-to-do people.[2]

---

[1] *Heritage Review*, Vols. 5 and 6, Mutschelknaus, Frederick, June 1973, pp. 4-6.

[2] *Heritage Review*, Vols. 5 and 6, Mutschelknaus, Frederick, June 1973, pp. 4-6.

Friedrich Mutschelknaus married **Karolina Delzer** on 3 October 1872. Karolina was born 13 May 1852 in Johannestal, South Russia.[1] Her parents were **Gottlieb** and **Barbara Staiger Delzer** who married in Rohrbach 20 May 1851.[2]

Friedrich Mutschelknaus filed his declaration of intent on 17 November 1879 in Yankton County.[3] Friedrich and Karolina Mutschelknaus had thirteen children—four sons and nine daughters. They homesteaded on the southwest quarter of section 32 in Odessa Township, but in 1875 moved to a farm near Freeman, Hutchinson County, Dakota Territory. Karolina died 7 April 1916 in Freeman.[4]

Gottlieb Mutschelknaus
Gottlieb Mutschelknaus was born 16 January 1854, in Johannestal, South Russia, to **Jakob** and **Rebecca Mutschelknaus**. Gottlieb came to America with his family aboard the *Tiger* in 1872. On 25 November 1877, Gottlieb married **Regina Kusler***, daughter of **Catharina Barbara Müller Diede Kussler Jasmann*** and **Johann Kussler**. Regina was born 25 February 1857. Gottlieb homesteaded on section 32. Their children were:

1. Gustoph b 8 October 1879
2. Jacob b 14 January 1881
3. Emil b 7 September 1883
4. Ema b 12 August 1885
5. Bertha b 20 January 1887
6. Karl b 9 April 1888
7. Johann b 1889
8. Julius b 20 March 1891

---

[1] Odessa Digital Library, St. Petersburg Archives, Rohrbach Birth Records, 185x (D. Wahl). http://pixel.cs.vt.edu/library/stpete/rohr/link/rohr185b.txt.

[2] Odessa Digital Library, St. Petersburg Archives, Rohrbach Marriage Records, 185x (D. Wahl). http://pixel.cs.vt.edu/library/stpete/rohr/link/rohr185m.txt.

[3] Odessa Digital Library, Yankton County SD Declarations of Intent (A. Brosz), http://pixel.cs.vt.edu/library/ships/link/yankton1.txt.

[4] *Heritage Review*, Volume 23, No. 1, March 1993, p. 31.

Jakob Mutschelknaus

Jakob Mutschelknaus, 46, his wife **Rebekka Müller**, 42, and their family were part of the second group of Germans to leave Russia on October 30, 1872.[1] **Friedrich Mutschelknaus** stated, "[t]his second party, leaving reaped their crops, threshed and sold them, and once at sea, the group experienced such a severe storm that it damaged their ship and forced them to turn back. After transferring all of the ship's passengers and goods onto the steamship *Tiger*, the group arrived in New York sometime after 2 December 1872.[2] (The second group's departure, ocean passage, and train trip are explained in Friedrich Mutschelknaus' biography.)

In the spring of 1873, the German-Russian group sent land spies to the western parts of North America to find enough land upon which all of them could live together. Jakob Mutschelknaus was part of the group that found and settled land in the area that would be called Odessa, in Yankton County, Dakota Territory.

Once in Yankton, Dakota Territory, Jakob Mutschelknaus bought horses and a wagon and drove across the land looking for a section on which to settle. After a few days, he decided on the northeast quarter of section 32 and the northwest quarter of section 33. Jakob's son, Friedrich Mutschelknaus, wrote an article for the *Dakota Freie Press* concerning the first groups to arrive in America. The following tells about his father's first year in Dakota:

> ...there were those in Sandusky who pitied us for wanting to go out to Dakota into the wilderness where they feared we would not make a living. We sowed the little land in the spring of 1874 that had been broken in 1873, and then in the month of July the heads were bounteously [sic] filled with grain. At that time, August Scheller, who also had pitied us so very much, came out from Sandusky for he was very inquisitive to see in what kind of wilderness his countrymen had settled. When he saw how abundantly the grain was standing and what kind of land we had, he said to my father, Jakob Mutschelknaus, "Jakob, you could not have found

[1] Rath, p. 63.
[2] Rath, pp. 61-62.

> anywhere in the United States a more suitable place for your vocation; and knowing German industry and thrift well, I do not hesitate a moment to say that here you will become well-to-do people.[1]

Jakob married Rebekka Müller 20 October 1850. Jakob was born to **Friedrich** and **(Jakobine) Barbara (Heinle) Mutschelknaus.** Friedrich was 28 and Barbara was 24 at the time of the Johannestal 1825 census. They had the following children at the time, Maria 2, Wilhelmine 1.[2] Friedrich Mutschelknaus died 27 January 1842 in Johannestal. The records show that he was 45 years, 4 months and 15 days when he died. He was born in Grossaschback, Wuerttemberg.[3] The 1860 Rohrbach death records state that Barbara Mutschelknaus was the widow of Friedrich, she died 4 August 1868 when she was 68, and she was born in Marbach, Wuerttemberg.[4]

According to the *Johannestal Beresan District Odessa 1858 Census,* Rebekka Müller is under her brother Christian Müller's family list as being absent since 1850. She is also listed with her husband Jakob Mutschelknaus as being 27 ears old. The couple had three children: Friedrich 5, Gottlieb 3, and Christina 1. Rebekka was the daughter of **Jakob Müller** and **Anna Maria Mühleisen.**

Jakob died in 1902 when he was 75. Rebekka Müller Mutschelknaus died in 1911 when she was 80.[5] They are both buried in the Odessa Lutheran Cemetery in Yankton County.

Reister
Michael Reister
Michael Reister claimed the northeast quarter of section 2. He was born in Russia circa 1833, arrived in 1874, and filed for naturalization on 16 November 1874.

---

[1] *Heritage Review*, Volumes 5 and 6, June 1973, p. 4.

[2] Stumpp, p. 715

[3] Odessa Digital Libaray, St. Petersburg Archives, Rohrbach Death Records, 184x (D. Wahl), http://pixel.cs.vt.edu/library/stpete/rohr/link/rohr1840d.txt

[4] Odessa Digital Libaray, St. Petersburg Archives, Rohrbach Death Records, 186x (D. Wahl), http://pixel.cs.vt.edu/library/stpete/rohr/link/rohr1860d.txt

[5] Odessa Digital Library, Yankton County, SD Cemeteries (E. Morrison). http://pixel.cs.vt.edu/cgi-bin/isearch.

The 1880 U.S. Federal Census shows that Reister was 46 years old, lived in the city of Yankton, his occupation was "merchant," and both of his parents were born in Wuerttemberg. His wife **Julia** claimed she was 41 years old, a housekeeper, born in Russia, and both her parents were born in Wuerttemberg. Julia could be **Juliana Frank** born 9 July 1838 in Neu Freudental to **Jacob Frank** and **Eva Margaretha Hauser.**[1]

The census also shows Michael and Julia had the following children living with them at the time:

1. Amelia 20, b in Russia
2. Robert 11, b in Russia
3. Beata 8, b in Russia
4. Theodore 1, b in Dakota

Rude
Anna Rude

Anna Rude filed for homestead rights to portions of the southeastern and southwestern quarters of section 12. She was born 1819 in Russia and arrived in America in 1875. On 8 February 1876 Anna filed for naturalization.

Georg Rude

Georg Rude applied for naturalization on 13 December 1875 in Yankton County. He was born in 1835 in Russia and came to America in 1875. He homesteaded on the northeast quarter of section 12. By the time the 1880 Federal Census was taken, Rude was 45 years old and lived with his wife **Jakobine (Hoffman)** who was 43. They had the following children:

1. Johann 19
2. Bernhardt (sp) 17
3. Margareth 15
4. Heinrich 13
5. Jakob 11
6. Jakobine 9

---

[1] Odessa Digital Library, St. Petersburg Archives, Freudental Birth Records, 183x (R. Wiseman). http://pixel.cs.vt.edu/library/stpete/freud/link/freu183b.txt.

7. Daniel 4
8. Georg b 24 October 1880

Johann Rude
Johann Rude homesteaded on the northwest quarter of section 12. He was married to **Carolina Haar.**
Some of their children include:

1. Gottlieb b 24 July 1889
2. Heinrich Edward b 11 April 1891
3. Wilhelmina Friedricka b 13 December 1892
4. Helena Maria b 1 March 1895
5. Solomon Georg b 9 January 1897
6. Johanna b 2 October 1898

Sailer (Saylor, Sayler, Sailor)
Andreas Sailer
   Andreas Sailer was born 7 October 1844 in Johannestal, South Russia, to **Johannes (2)** and **Anna Maria Bette Sailer.**[1]
   According to Stumpp's *The Emigration from Germany to Russia in the Years 1763 to 1862*, Johannes Sailer (2) was born circa 1800 to **Johannes (1)** and **Anna Barbara Sayler** of Dornstetten/ Feudenstadt-Wuerttemberg. Johannes (1) was born circa 1778 and Anna Barbara was born circa 1788. The family arrived in Russia in 1817. By the 1825 census for Johannestal, Johannes (1) was 47, Barbara 37, Johannes (2) 17, Friedrich 10, Gottlieb 8, Rosina 2.[2]
   The 1850 Rohrbach death files state that Johannes Sayler (1) died in Johannestal on 21 November 1855. He was 78 years, 28 days of age, and Lutheran. The 1870 Rohrbach death files state that Anna Barbara died 7 June 1874. She was 87 years, 1 month, 22 days old and had been born in Dornstetten, Germany.[3] The records also state that she was the widow of Johannes Sailer (1).

[1] Odessa Digital Library, St. Petersburg Archives, Rohrbach Birth Records, 184x (D. Wahl). http://pixel.cs.vt.edu/library/stpete/rohr/link/rohr184b.txt.
[2] Stumpp, p. 714.
[3] Odessa Digital Library, St. Petersburg Archives, Rohrbach Death Records, 187x (D. Wahl). http://pixel.cs.vt.edu/library/stpete/rohr/link/rohr187d.txt.

The Rohrbach birth and death records indicate that Johannes (2) and Anna Maria Bette had the following children during the years 1830-1858:

1. Jakob Friedrich b 13 July 1833, Johannestal, SR, d 21 Nov. 1844, 11 yrs
2. Gottlieb (Sayler) b 8 April 1836, Johannestal, SR
3. M Barbara Heinle Ullmer[1]
4. Ludwig b 16 May 1838, Johannestal, SR, d 28 Dec. 1844
5. Johannes b 13 July 1840
6. Michael b 2 October 1842
7. Andreas b 7 October 1844, Johannestal, SR
8. Mattheus b 29 Dec. 1846, Johannestal, SR
9. Christine b 6 June 1854, Johannestal, SR
10. Carolina b 20 Dec. 1856, Johannestal, SR, d 21 April 1858

Andreas age 28, his wife **Catherine** age 28 (Christina Katie according to 1880 census), and children Ludwig 6, Christina 4, Andreas 1 1/2, and Anna 1/4, left Hamburg, traveling to Hull. They then traveled overland to Liverpool, boarded their ship, and arrived in New York on October 30, 1872.

Andreas Sayler and family belonged to the second group of Germans to leave Russia.[2] This group experienced a severe storm on the North Sea. The ship was badly damaged and turned back to England so the passengers could board a different vessel. After they had been at sea thirty-six days on the steamship *Tiger*, crew and passengers arrived at their destination: "The second group landed in New York after the 2nd of December. It was in Sandusky between the 10th and 15th of December, 1872."[3]

After wintering in Sandusky, the Andreas Sayler family moved to Odessa Township, Yankton County, Dakota Territory, and homesteaded on the northwest quarters of sections 21 and 23.

Andreas Sayler applied for and received his naturalization papers on 23 June 1879. According to the 1880 U.S. Federal Census, Andreas and Catherine (Christina Katie) had additional children:

---

[1] *History of Yankton County,* p. 647.

[2] *Heritage Review*, Volume 15, September, 1976, p. 15.

[3] Ibid.

1. Rosina 5
2. Elizabeth 3
3. Christian 2

The same census states that Andreas' parents were born in Germany. Catherina's parents were born in Wuerttemberg. By the 1910 U.S. Federal Census, the northwest quarter of section 21 was owned by **Heinrich Weidenbach, Jr.**, and the northwest quarter of section 23 was owned by **August Hermann**.

Ludwig Sayler

    Ludwig Sayler was born circa 16 May 1838 to **Johannes (2)** and **Anna (Justina) Bette Sayler** of Johannestal, South Russia (see Andreas Sailer notes).[1] Ludwig married **Friedericka Heinle** on 2 March 1859.[2] Friedericka was born 12 December 1837 in Johannestal to **Christian Heinle** and **Anna Maria Zimmerman**.[3] The St. Petersburg birth records for Rohrbach in the 1860's indicate that Ludwig and Friedericka Sayler had the following children:

1. Ludwig b 25 May 1860, Johannestal
2. Rosine b 12 March 1862, Johannestal
3. Karoline b 13 Jan. 1864, Johannestal
4. Johann b 13 Aug. 1868, Johannestal

    According to the 1880 U.S. Federal Census, Ludwig claimed that his parents were both born in Wuerttemburg, Germany.

    Ludwig Sayler and his family belonged to the second group that left Russia in October of 1872.[4] Following their winter stay in Sandusky, in the spring of 1873, he, his wife Fredericka and their children moved to Dakota Territory and homesteaded on the northwest and southwest quarters of section 35 in Odessa Township.

---

[1] Odessa Digital Library, St. Petersburg Archives, Rohrbach Birth Records, 183x (D. Wahl). http://pixel.cs.vt.edu/library/stpete/rohr/link/rohr183b.txt.

[2] Odessa Digital Library, St. Petersburg Archives, Rohrbach Marriage Records, 185x (D. Wahl). http://pixel.cs.vt.edu/library/stpete/rohr/link/rohr185m.txt.

[3] Odessa Digital Library, St. Petersburg Archives, Rohrbach Birth Records, 183x (D. Wahl). http://pixel.cs.vt.edu/library/stpete/rohr/link/rohr183b.txt.

[4] See chapter on Friedrich Mutschelknaus.

On 16 September 1882, Ludwig was a witness for Friedrich Frank when Friedrich proved-up on his homestead. Ludwig was also a witness for Friedrich's brother Andreas Frank when he proved-up on his homestead 27 September 1883.

An article in the *Lesterville Ledger* dated 10 February 1891 states the following about Sayler:

> **Lesterville is having a little post office war. Ludwig Saylor was promised the position for political services last fall, and the citizens are protesting against his appointment.**

The following children belonged to Ludwig and Fredericka Sayler (ages according to the 1880 U.S. Federal Census and cemetery records):

1. Ludwig 20, d 20 June 1933, buried St. Petersburg Cemetery, Odessa Township
2. Rosina 18
3. Carolina 16
4. Christian 14
5. Johann 12, d 20 April 1937, buried St. Petersburg Cemetery, Odessa Township
6. Heinrich 5
7. Magdalena 3

Ludwig Sayler died in 1892. He is buried in the Odessa Lutheran Cemetery on section 28 of Odessa Township.

Mattaus Sailer
    Mattaus (Mathaeus) Sailer was born 29 December 1846 in Johannestal to **Johann (2)** and **Anna Sailer** (see Andreas Sailer notes on parentage).[1] On 24 November 1868, he married **(Anna) Marie Diede** who was born 7 March 1850 to **Gottlieb** and **Anna Margarethe Müller Diede**.[2] Stumpp acknowledges in the 1825

---

[1] Odessa Digital Library, St. Petersburg Archives, Rohrbach Birth Records, 184x (D. Wahl). http://pixel.cs.vt.edu/library/stpete/rohr/link/rohr184b.txt.

[2] Odessa Digital Library, St. Petersburg Archives, Rohrbach Birth Records, 185x (D. Wahl). http://pixel.cs.vt.edu/library/stpete/rohr/link/rohr185b.txt.

census for Johannestal that Gottlieb Diede was 8 when he, along with father Michael 32, mother Anna Christina 31, and his siblings, Michael 2, and Anna Christine 6, arrived in Johannestal in 1819. According to the St. Petersburg files, the Diedes were married 8 June 1837 in Johannestal[1] and had the following children born in Johannestal:

1. Anna Christina b 31 May 1838
2. Johann Gottlieb b 21 Jan. 1840 d. 14 July 1840, 6 months old
3. Johann Jacob b 27 Dec. 1841
4. Maria Dorothea b 7 Oct. 1843
5. Carolina b 11 Aug. 1845
6. Michael b 7 Dec. 1847, d Oct. 1859, 11 years 10 months 20 d
7. Anna Maria b 7 March 1850
8. Catharina b 8 March 1852
9. Margaretha b 7 Feb. 1854
10. Heinrich b 4 Feb. 1856
11. Christian b 4 May 1858
12. Regine b 18 June 1862
13. Rosine b 13 Feb. 1865
14. Gottlieb b 26 Feb. 1868

Mattaus, Anna Maria, and the rest of the Sailer family were part of the first group to leave Russia in the summer of 1872. According to George Rath in *The Black Sea Germans in the Dakotas*, "they had great difficulties to overcome in getting their documents since they were the first emigrants."[2] After the secretary of the village had first filled out all of the necessary papers, they had to get documents from Nikolajew, Odessa, and Cherson before they could depart. Because of the hindrances, "the matter was put off to such an extent that the first ones could leave only a short time before the second group."[3]

Although the passenger list states that these first individuals were leaving Odessa, South Russia, and were farm-hands, "all of them came from Johannestal and were not mere farm-hands, as

---

[1] Odessa Digital Library, St. Petersburg Archives, Rohrbach Marriage Records, 183x, (D. Wahl). http://pixel.cs.vt.edu/library/stpete/rohr/link/rohr183m.txt.

[2] Rath, pp. 60-61.

[3] Ibid.

recorded, but landowners."[1]

Along with Mattaus, his wife Marie, and their children, many of his relatives, including his father and mother Johannes and Anna Sailer, his sisters Christiana and Christine, and a brother Philip also left Russia. They boarded at Hamburg, Germany, on the steamship *British Queen.*

Once they arrived in America, they traveled to Sandusky, Ohio, and stayed the winter with **Ludwig Bette**, a well-to-do relative who had left Russia in 1848 and eventually settled on Kellys Island, Ohio.

After the scouts returned with information about available land in Dakota Territory, Mattaus Sailer and his family took up a homestead on the southeast quarters of sections 34 and 35 in Odessa Township, Yankton County.

The following children of Mattaus and Maria were listed on the ship list:

1. Johannes 2, b 30 Nov. 1869
2. Christine ½, b 17 Dec. 1871

By the 1880 U.S. Federal Census, the Sailers also had the following children:

3. Elizabeta 5
4. Heinrich 3
5. Maethaeu 1

Schaefer
Heinrich Schaefer

Heinrich Schaefer and family came to Odessa Township from Johannestal, South Russia, in 1874. He was born 25 December 1831. Schaefer married **Magdalena Eissinger** 25 January 1853.[2] Magdalena was born 10 October 1833 to **Johannes** and **Catharina Eissinger**.[3]

---

[1] Rath, pp. 60-61.

[2] Odessa Digital Library, St. Petersburg Archives, Rohrbach Marriage Records, 185x (D. Wahl). http://pixel.cs.vt.edu/library/stpete/rohr/link/rohr185m.txt.

[3] Odessa Digital Library, St. Petersburg Archives, Rohrbach Birth Records, 183x (D. Wahl). http://pixel.cs.vt.edu/library/stpete/rohr/link/rohr183b.txt.

STEPPES TO NEU ODESSA   85

On 23 July 1873 the Heinrich Schaefer family arrived in New York aboard the vessel *Westphalia* that sailed from Hamburg, Germany.

Son of **Valentin** and **Maria Schaefer**, Heinrich homesteaded on the southwest quarter of section 31. Heinrich and Magdalena were members of the German Reformed Odessa Church. The following children are listed in the records of that church:

1. Johannes b 24 March 1854, m Fredericka Saylor in 1877 (b 12 August 1858, Johannestal, SR), imm 1878 from Johannestal, SR. They had 15 children, homesteaded in Lincoln Township, section 1, Bon Homme County, DT, church membership with the St. Petersburg Lutheran Church
2. Adam b 16 November 1855, m Elizabeth Reich 1878 (b 16 November 1858), imm 1880 from Johannestal, SR, d 1911 at the age of 55, buried in St. Petersburg Cemetery, Odessa Township
3. Susanna b 16 April 1858, d 14 Feb. 1863
4. Maria b 22 January 1861
5. Karl b 22 May 1866, m Magdalena Schempp 4 December 1888
6. Magdalena b 25 April 1869
7. Susanna b 22 February 1872

Magdalena Eissinger Schaefer died 30 October 1906 at the age of 73. She is buried at the St. Petersburg Cemetery in Odessa Township.

Valentin Schaefer
Valentin Schaefer was born in Godramstein, Bavaria, Germany, on 27 August 1806. His father was **Christoph Schaefer** who was born in 1773 in Bavaria, Germany.[1]

Schaefer and his wife **Anna Maria Schatz**, who was born circa 1803, had a number of children while living in Johannestal, South Russia. St. Petersburg records for Rohrbach indicate a number of other children were born after 1830.

1. Adam b 4 July 1834
2. Eva Catharina b 31 December 1836 d 26 February 1837
3. Eva Catharina b 10 June 1838

[1] Kusler, pp. 11-15.

4. Rosine b 28 December 1840 (see Jacob Auch)*
5. Jacob b 1 March 1843 d 22 July 1844
6. Jacob born b 19 April 1845
7. Christine b 15 June 1847

In 1872 the Schaefers left Johannestal along with other members from the second group and came to America where they settled for the winter in Sandusky, Ohio. In the spring of 1873, the Schaefers arrived in Dakota Territory. Valentin "first took out a homestead in section 1 of Bon Homme County. He later relinquished that land and took a claim in the SW 1/4 of Section 31 in Odessa Township, Yankton County."[1]

Valentin Schaefer received his naturalization papers in 1880. His "homestead papers reveal that in May 1883 he sold his homestead and went to live with his daughter, **Christina Kusler**, who lived about 3/4 of a mile from his homestead."[2] Valentin Schaefer died 19 September 1894.

Schamber
Johannes (Johann, John) Schamber

"Back in the late 1700's one **Ludweg Chambre**, French army officer in Alsace-Lorraine, wanted to migrate to Russia. But he was not eligible. He left his service to France, moved into nearby Switzerland, forsook his Catholic faith for Lutheran and changed his name to the German-sounding **Schamber**. Now going into Germany he could migrate to Crimea as a German farmer, which he did in 1803."[3]

According to the Neusatz death records for 1840, **Ludwig Schamber** was born circa 1798 in Kerberg, Lothringen. He first settled in Friedenthal, Crimea, where he and his wife, **Christina Traxel**, who are listed as in the birth records as "father reformist and mother Lutheran," had a number of children. The following are listed in the 1830 and 1840 Neusatz birth and death records of the St. Petersburg files:

---

[1] Kusler, pp. 11-15.
[2] Ibid.
[3] Wagner, *Daughters of Dakota*, pp. 15-18.

1. Catharina b 28 May 1833, died 8 Oct. 1840
2. Rosina b 19 Sept. 1835
3. Martin b 23 Nov. 1837
4. Conrad b 23 Dec. 1839
5. daughter b 13 Aug. 1842, d 13 Aug. 1842
6. Sophie b 8 July 1843

Ludwig Schamber died 25 November 1844. In the Neusatz records, Schamber is listed as a "Colonial of Friedenthal."
Three of his grown children, Peter (1) (who is not listed in the St. Petersburg files) and his family, Martin and his family, and Margaret came to America and settled in Dakota.[1]
The St. Petersburg records for Neusatz indicate that **Johannes Schamber** was born 23 February 1856 to **Peter Schamber (1)** and **Wilhelmina Liese** (spelling variation: Leusi, Linse, Lousi) who settled in Odessa Township on sections 2 and 3. In 1874 Johannes Schamber and his uncle **Martin Schamber** "emigrated to the USA to seek their fortune."[2] He filed for naturalization 20 November 1874. He then settled in Odessa Township on the northern half of the southwest quarter of section 2 and the northern half of the southeast quarter of section 3. His uncle Martin Schamber settled across the county line in Sweet Township, Hutchinson County, on the southern half of section 35.
Two articles in *The Hutchinson Citizen* state the following about Johannes Schamber:

24 April 1890 - A lively run-away occurred in town last **Saturday.** A team, with buggy attached, belonging to **John Schamber** was standing tied with the lines a dangerous run-strap when they became frightened and broke away. They made it a point to call on most of our citizens, in their way, and then took to the prairie. But by this time they were about run down and several parties overtook them on the hill north of town and caught them. No damage was done whatsoever, except the breaking of both lines. The team ran through a grove of timber, but luckily every tree was missed.

---
[1] *MENNO*, pp. 573-576.
[2] Ibid.

28 August 1890 - John Schamber and Jacob Schnaidt left on Friday last for Pierre, where they go to look at the city, and view the "barren waste" west of Pierre, better known perhaps, as the Sioux reservation. When they return our people will be able to learn definitely as to the true character of the soil and resources of that portion of the state which has been so grossly misrepresented by the people who are laboring for the cause of Huron for the permanent capital. If they were not laboring in a cause directly in conflict with the best interests of the whole state, they would not be compelled to resort to measures so questionable.

Johann Schamber and his family are listed in the 1900 Federal Census for Hutchinson County. The records state that he was born March 1856. He was 44, married for 19 years, born in Russia and both parents were born in Russia. He came to America in 1874, and his occupation was state's treasurer. His wife **Maria** was born December 1862. She was 37, had given birth to 10 children of which 8 were still living. Both she and her parents had been born in Russia and she came to America in 1878. The following records indicate the couple's children still living at home, their birth months and years, and their ages:

1. Adolph b Sept. 1882; 17
2. Robert b Dec. 1883; 16
3. Otto b Aug. 1885; 14
4. Hildegard b Sept. 1887; 12
5. Hertha b Aug. 1889; 10
6. Edgar b Aug. 1894; 5
7. Udo b Feb. 1897; 3
8. Helwig; b Nov. 1898; 1

The 1910 U.S. Federal Census for Hutchinson County lists a few more Schamber children.

9. Hatiovck (sp) 11 (daughter)
10. Bechtold (sp) 8 (son)
11. Alfred 6

Johann Schamber's land, located on section 2, was owned by **Otilla Hertz**; his land on section 3 was owned by **Peter Schamber.**

Peter Schamber (1)

On 16 July 1875, **Peter Schamber (1)** was met by his brother **Martin Schamber** at the railroad station in Yankton. He had left the Crimea with his wife **Wilhelmina** (Liese, Leusi, or Lousi), their six children, including three married children and their spouses, and a "sister of Peter I, Margaret, either came with them or came later."[1]

According to the Yankton County Naturalization records, Schamber was born in Russia in 1828. He filed for naturalization on 22 July 1875. He then homesteaded in Odessa Township on the southern half of the northeast quarter of section 3, the northern half of the southwest quarter of section 3, and the southern half of the northwest quarter of section 2 "one mile east and five miles south of Menno in the hills near the James River bottoms. The family lived in a sodhouse which became the home for the entire group of Schamber immigrants."[2]

While one son named Johannes Schamber (see Johannes Schamber biography) had immigrated earlier with Peter's brother Martin, a daughter and son-in-law, **Joseph** and **Rosina Schamber Bohrer**, arrived and settled across the Yankton County line in Sweet Township, Hutchinson County, on section 33. Another son, **Peter Schamber (2)** and his wife **Susan Weidner**,[3] also homesteaded in Odessa Township in sections 2, 3, and 10.

According to 1850 and 1860 St. Petersburg birth and death files for Neusatz, **Peter** and **Wilhelmina Schamber** had the following children who were born in Russia:

1. Catharina b 30 Jan. 1850 Friedenthal
2. Peter b 3 Sept. 1851 Friedenthal
3. Rosine b 28 Feb. 1854 Friedenthal
4. Johannes b 23 Feb. 1856 Friedenthal
5. Johannes Georg b 6 Dec. 1858 Friedenthal
6. Elizabeth b 5 May 1861 Friedenthal
7. Wilhelmina b 25 Feb. 1864 Neuzats, d 13 April 1866

---

[1] Wagner, pp. 16-18.

[2] *MENNO*, pp. 573-576.

[3] Wagner, p. 16.

8. Son b 14 Jan. 1868 Neusatz d 14 Jan. 1868

According to the 1880 U.S. Federal Census for Yankton County, **(Johannes) Peter Schamber (1)** was 51, his occupation was "farmer," he was born in Russia, his father was born in Prussia, and his mother was born in Wuerttemberg. **Wilhelmina** was 53, her occupation was "wife," her father was born in Switzerland, and her mother was born in Austria. They had three children at home: Johannes, 24; George, 21; Elizabeth, 19. "Hutchinson County, SD Cemeteries" for Grand View Cemetery near Freeman, South Dakota, indicate a "Willma" Schamber died in 1884.[1]

By the 1900 U.S.Federal Census for Hutchinson County, Peter Schamber claimed he was born October 1828, and that he was 71. The records indicate that he had married a second time. His wife **Anna** claimed she was 62, born January 1838 and the mother of 11 children, of which 5 were still living. She stated that she was born in Russia, but both parents were born in Germany. She also claimed that she had been in the United States for 15 years, having arrived in 1885.

Peter died in 1901 when he was 73.[2] Anna was 72 and living alone, according to the 1910 U.S. Federal Census for Hutchinson County.

By 1910 **Gustav Gunderson** owned Peter's land that was part of the southwest quarter of section 3, and Peter's grandson **George Schamber** owned the portion of his land that was in section 2.

Peter Schamber (2)

Peter Schamber (2), son of Peter Schamber (1), was born in 3 September 1851 in Friedenthal, Crimea. Susana Weidner, born in 1856 at Krohnenthal, Crimea, worked for the elder Schambers "from childhood through her teens. At the age of eighteen, **Susana Weidner** was married to Peter (2)."[3]

On 26 May 1875, the young Schambers left Russia and sailed to America. Peter applied for naturalization on 22 July 1875. He and

[1] Odessa Digital Library, Hutchinson County SD Cemeteries (E. Morrison). http://pixel.cs.vt.edu/library/cemeteries/sodak/link/hutchsd.txt.
[2] Ibid.
[3] *MENNO*, pp. 573-576.

Susana homesteaded on the southern half of the northeast quarter of section 3, the southern half of the southwest quarter of section 2, and the northern half of the northeast quarter of section 10 in Odessa Township, Yankton County where he and Susana "built their sod home in a low place beside a creek that emptied into the James River and moved in that fall. It was a rolling piece of land, foothills of the James."[1]

Schamber "experimented with the planting of an apple orchard. Soon he had a supply of apples for family, relatives, friends and neighbors."[2] Peter also "built sod barns for cows, sheep, and horses."[3]

Susana "had a quiet, uncomplaining disposition, stout heartedly carrying on her duties as wife and mother, rearing the children in the faith of her fathers." She cooked, sewed, cleaned, gardened and helped with whatever farm work she could handle. One time while milking a cow, a ram hit her from behind. As a result, she broke her collarbone. Since she did not have access to medical help for her injury, the "break healed in time but left her somewhat stooped and crippled. The grandchildren knew her as the little crippled grandmother."[4]

Peter Schamber and his family "lived on the hilly farm from 1875 until 1907."[5] They moved into Menno, Hutchinson County, South Dakota, where they lived until 1912. When Peter was sixty-one, he "made a trip to the Bitterroot Valley in western Montana, where he bought some land that was to be irrigated." He came back to Dakota and "sold the Menu [sic] home and moved with Susana and Pauline, to Stevensville, Montana. There he raised oats, alfalfa, other small grains, plus apples and cherries from his orchard."[6]

The Schambers lived in Montana until 1929.[7] They moved back to South Dakota and lived by their son near Freeman "where George

---

[1] MENNO, pp. 573-576.
[2] Ibid.
[3] Wagner, pp. 16-18.
[4] Ibid.
[5] Ibid.
[6] Wagner, pp. 16-18.
[7] Ibid.

built a small house for them."[1] Susana died 9 June 1932. Peter Schamber died 12 February 1936. Both are buried in the Menno Cemetery, Menno, South Dakota.

Peter Schamber (2) and **Susana Weidner Schamber** had the following children:

1. Wilhelmina b 1 February 1876, m Henry Frasch
2. Regina b 22 July 1878, m John Preszler
3. George b 12 November 1879, m Hellen Stoller
4. Bertha b 3 September 1884, m August Schorzman
5. Helen b 14 March 1881, d 1899
6. Clara b 21 February, m Emil Ulmer

"All were baptized and confirmed in the Lutheran faith."[2]

Schorzman
Johann Schorzman

Johann Schorzman (Schotzmann, Schorzmann, Schortzman) was born 1 April 1853 in Russia.[3] Schorzman and his brother **Heinrich**, who was born 03 August 1850, departed from Odessa, Russia, in the fall of 1872 and boarded the steamship *Tiger* on 5 November 1872. Heinrich settled in Lesterville Township.

Johann and Heinrich Schorzman's father **Johann Adam Schorzman Sr.** was born in 1817 in Germany "and left Wittenburg [*sic*] with his parents some years later to look for more land. The family came with other families to Russia in horse-drawn wagons with their belongings and lived in dugouts and sod houses until towns were developed." Here also, similar to the future generations that would homestead in Dakota Territory, "their homes were built of bricks made from straw and clay and dried in the sun."[4] Stumpp's *The Emigration from Germany to Russia in the Years 1763-1862* shows "deren Mann Johann Schotzmann" came to Johannestal, South Russia, from Ossweil, Ludwigsburg, Wuerttemberg in 1818

---

[1] *MENNO*, p. 574.

[2] Wagner, pp. 16-18.

[3] Odessa Digital Library, St. Petersburg Archives, Rohrbach Birth Records, 185x (D. Wahl). http://pixel.cs.vt.edu/library/stpete/rohr/link/rohr185b.txt.

[4] *MENNO*, p. 566.

with son Johann Adam 1, Barbara 10, and wife **Margareta** 23. Margareta's father, Andreas Hagenlocher, who was 60, also came.[1] According to the St. Petersburg records, **Margareta Hagenlocker Schortzman** (Maria Margaretha) died 21 September 1860 in Johannestal, South Russia. Johann was 64 when he died on 4 January 1856. The death records also state that he was born in Duschin, Germany.[2] In addition to the children listed in Stumpp's text, the 1830 Rohrbach birth records also list the following children born to **Johann** and **Maria Mararetha Hagenlocker Schortzman**:

1. Magdalena b 3 Jan 1835
2. Rosina b 17 Jan 1838 d 13 Nov 1838
3. Christian b 31 Aug 1839

Johann Adam Schorzman married **Anna Mueller** 9 November 1843 in Rohrbach, Russia.[3] Anna Mueller was born 18 July 1826 in Johannestal, South Russia. There are a number of children listed in the 1840 Rohrbach birth records as being born to either Johann or Johannes Schorzman. Since there were at least three individuals with similar names and no wives' names listed for the children who were born, identification for specific family members has been difficult. But between the St. Petersburg files for Rohrbach and *MENNO: The First Hundred Years 1879-1979*, the consensus could be made that **Johann Adam** and **Anna Mueller Schorzman** had the following children:

1. Johann Jacob (later referred to as Jacob) b 27 Oct 1844
2. Johannestal d 13 May 1931 m Christine Ulmer
3. Caroline b 22 March 1847 d 24 March 1847
4. Catharina b 28 Feb 1848 d 18 Oct 1859
5. Heinrich b 08 Aug 1850 m Mathilda Stoller
6. Johann b 1 April 1853 m Christine Barth
7. Margareth b 27 June 1855 m Peter Seydel

---

[1] Stumpp, p. 714.

[2] Odessa Digital Library, St. Petersburg Archives, Rohrbach Death Records, 185x (D. Wahl). http://pixel.cs.vt.edu/library/stpete/rohr/link/rohr185d.txt.

[3] Odessa Digital Library, St. Petersburg Archives, Rohrbach Marriage Records, 184x (D. Wahl). http://pixel.cs.vt.edu/library/stpete/rohr/link/rohr184m.txt.

8. Christian b 9 March 1858 d 6 Jan 1945 m Christina Ulmer[1]

Oral tradition states Johann Adam and one of his sons were kidnapped by the Cossacks on or around 1860 and taken to Siberia.[2] After Johann Adam's disappearance, **Anna Mueller Schorzman** married **Karl Lutz** on 18 February 1864 in Johannesthal.[3] Lutz' first marriage was to **Jacobine Martin** who died 16 October 1863. Even though Lutz' death is not registered in the St. Petersburg files, *MENNO: The First 100 Years 1879-1979* does not list him as coming to America.

Anna Schorzman left Russia at age 48 and came to America with at least three of her other children: Christ 14, Margaret 18, Jacob 29; Jacob's wife Christine 27, and their son Gottlieb 6, and daughters Catherine 3 and Louise 9 months. After arriving in America aboard the *Westphalia* on 23 July 1873, the family stayed in Sandusky, Ohio, for the rest of the summer and the following winter. Their stay in Ohio created a clash of cultures because "their foreign dress drew taunts from the local children, prompting snowball fights between the American and the foreign youngsters."[4] The following year the Schorzman family boarded a train for Dakota Territory where "they stayed in barracks built by the railroad company. Soon they built sod houses, and in later years, hauled lumber from Yankton for more modern dwellings."[5]

Johann Schorzman married **Christina Barth**.[6] His homestead land consisted of the southwest quarter of the southwest quarter of section 18.

Johann and **Christine Barth Schorzman** had the following children:

1. John m Emelia Berreth
2. Jacob m Katherine Guthmiller
3. August m Pauline Schamber

---

[1] *MENNO*, p. 566.

[2] *MENNO*, p. 565.

[3] Odessa Digital Library, St. Petersburg Archives, Rohrbach Marriage Records, 186x (D. Wahl). http://pixel.cs.vt.edu/library/stpete/rohr/link/rohr186m.txt.

[4] *MENNO*, p. 566.

[5] Ibid.

[6] *MENNO*, p. 566.

4. Louise m Jacob Heckenliable
5. David m Christine Neuharth
6. Emelia m Ben Haar
7. Andrew m Meta Diede
8. Johanna m Christian Neuharth
9. Margret m Emil Jungman
10. Christiana m Frank Holt
11. Julius m Margaret Guthmiller
12. Theodore d in infancy

Johann Schorzman's mother, **Anna Mueller Schorzman**, died 23 November 1905 in Menno, South Dakota. By 1910 **Gottlieb Ulmer** owned **Johann Schorzman's** tract of land.

Schramm
Heinrich Schramm
Heinrich Schramm homesteaded on a western portion of sections 13 and 14. The 1880 U.S. Federal Census shows that Heinrich was 32, and he and his parents were born in Russia. His wife **Christina** was 31, born in Russia, and both of her parents were born in Wuerttemberg. According to the Yankton County Declaration of Intent, Schramm applied for naturalization 2 February 1885. Census records indicate that the Schramms have the following children living with them:

1. Jacobina 9
2. Jakob 8
3. Phillipina 6
4. Margareth 4
5. Johann 10/12

According to 1910 U.S. Federal Census, the Schramms lived in Mercer County, South Dakota. Heinrich was 63, Christina was 62, and they had two children still living with them, Ferdinand P, 20, and Ida Theresa, 10. The census also states that Heinrich and family came to America in 1875. Heinrich and Christina's son Jacob and his family were also living in Mercer County. The records show that he was 38, his wife Pauline was 37, Eduard was 14, Herbert was 12,

Johann was 11, and Emma was 8. The records state that Jacob came to America in 1876. By 1910 **George Mueller** owned Schramm's original homestead land.

Serr
Michael Serr

Michael Serr was born in Worms, South Russia, in 13 September 1839 to **Johann Christoph** and **Johanna (Hanna) Kost Serr** of Rhineland, Pfalz, Germany.

The St. Petersburg birth and death records for the years 1830-1870 state **Johann** and **Hanna** had the following children:

1. Jacob b 3 Feb 1833, Worms
2. Christoph b 7 July 1835, Worms
3. Georg d 30 May 1836, Worms, 1 year old
4. Christina b 10 Aug 1837, Worms, d 18 Nov 1838, 1 year
5. Michael b 13 Sept 1839, Worms
6. Christina b Jan 1842, Worms
7. George Peter d 9 Feb 1844, Worms, 14 days
8. Christian b 18 Jan. 1846, Worms, d 5 July 1847, 1 year 5 months
9. Johann b 31 Oct 1848, d 23 July 1848, Gueldendorf, 10 months 4 days

Johanna (Hanna) Kost Serr died 3 May 1877 in Worms. She was 71 years 10 months and 11 days.

There are conflicting dates for the marriage of **Michael Serr** and **Katharina Engel**. The St. Petersburg marriage records for the 1860's have two dates listed: 27 November 1860 and 29 December 1860. Katharina was born 21 March 1843 at Neu-Danzig, South Russia. Her parents were **Johann** and **Elizabeth Berndt Engel.***

On 23 July 1873, the Serrs, along with Katherina's parents, some of her sisters and their families, and other unmarried siblings, arrived in New York aboard the *Westphalia*. From New York the families boarded a train for Yankton County. In Yankton Serr applied for naturalization and a homestead. His homestead land consisted of the southwest quarter of section 26, the southeast quarter of section 27, and the northeast quarter of section 34 in

Odessa Township. Michael received his naturalization papers in 1879.

When the Serrs left Russia, they had been able to sell their property so that when they came to America they had approximately $5000. In turn, they were able to buy more land than the homestead grants allowed.

In 1887 Michael and Katharina deeded part of their land, the northeast section of 34, to be used for the Hoffnung Reformed Church of which Michael was one of the original organizers.

The Serrs continued to farm the rest of their land, and they became well known in the surrounding communities. The following article came from *The Scotland Journal*, 13 April 1895:

> **Michael Serr's wagon with a load of dirt became stuck in a mud hole on Railway Street Tuesday. For a while it looked as if there wasn't horses enough in town to pull the wagon out of its lodgement, if they had not unloaded the dirt.**

Around 1910 Michael and Katharina Serr moved to Portland, Oregon. Later they farmed near Wheeler, Grant County, Washington. Finally, they moved to Plevna, Fallon County, Montana, where their daughter **Rosina Serr Stoller** lived.

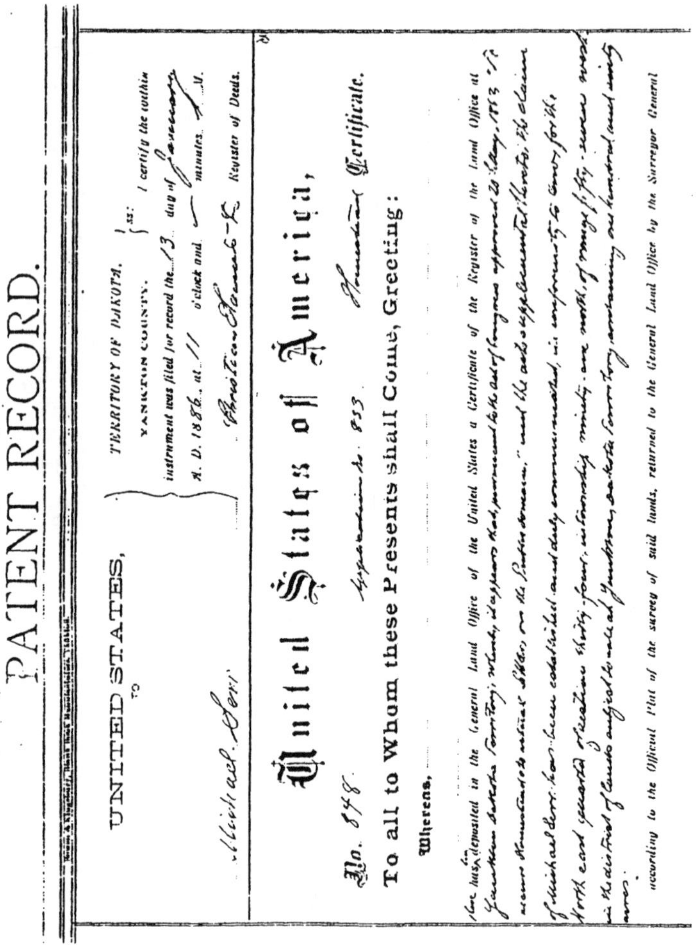
PATENT RECORD.

UNITED STATES,
TO
Michael Serr

TERRITORY OF DAKOTA, } ss:
YANKTON COUNTY.
I certify the within instrument was filed for record the 13 day of January A. D. 1886, at 11 o'clock and — minutes A. M.
Christian Hauck [illegible] Register of Deeds.

United States of America,

No. 848 Application No. 853 Homestead Certificate.

To all to Whom these Presents shall Come, Greeting:

Whereas, there has been deposited in the General Land Office of the United States a Certificate of the Register of the Land Office at Yankton Dakota Territory, whereby it appears that, pursuant to the Act of Congress approved 20 May, 1862 "To secure Homesteads to actual Settlers on the Public domain," and the acts supplemental thereto, the claim of Michael Serr has been established and duly consummated, in conformity to law, for the North east quarter of section thirty-four, in township ninety-one north, of range fifty-seven west in the district of lands subject to sale at Yankton, Dakota Territory, containing one hundred and sixty acres.

according to the Official Plat of the survey of said lands, returned to the General Land Office by the Surveyor General

Now Know Ye, That there is therefore granted by the United States unto the said *the above*

*[...] the tract of Land above described: To have and to hold the said tract of Land, with the appurtenances thereof, unto the said *Heirs and Ass[...]*

and to _____ *him* _____ heirs and assigns forever; subject to any vested and accrued water rights for mining, agricultural, manufacturing or other purposes, and rights to ditches and reservoirs used in connection with such water rights, as may be recognized and acknowledged by the local customs, laws and decisions of Courts, and also subject to the right of the proprietor of a vein or lode to extract and remove his ore therefrom, should the same be found to penetrate or intersect the premises hereby granted, as provided by law.

In Testimony Whereof, I, _____ *Rutherford B. Hayes* _____

President of the United States of America, have caused these letters to be made Patent and the Seal of the General Land Office to be thereunto affixed.

Given under my hand at the City of Washington, the _____ *Tenth* _____ day of _____ *December* _____ in the year of Our Lord One Thousand Eight Hundred and _____ *Eighty* _____ and of the Independence of the United States the One Hundredth and _____ *fifth* _____

By the President, _____ *R. B. Hayes*

By _____ *Wm W Curtis* _____ Secretary.

_____ *S. W. Clark* _____
Recorder for the General Land Office.

Recorded Vol. _____ *2* _____ Page _____ *392* _____

Michael Serr's Land Patent Record.

WARRANTY DEED RECORD.

This Indenture Made the _First_ day of _Gilbert_ in the Year of Our Lord One Thousand Eight Hundred and _Eighty seven_ by and between _Michael Sess_ and _Katharina Sess his wife_

of the County of _Hamilton_ in the Territory of Dakota, party of the first part, and _Hoffenweyer_ _Reformed Church Society_ of the County of _Hamilton_ in the _Row of dakota_ party of the second part: WITNESSETH, That the said part_y_ of the first part, for and in consideration of the sum of _One_ _____ DOLLARS, to _him_ in hand paid by the said part_y_ of the second part, the receipt whereof is hereby acknowledged, ha_s_ Granted, Bargained, Sold and Conveyed, and by three presents do_es_ Grant, Bargain, Sell and Convey unto the said part_y_ of the second part, _____ all _that_ certain piece or parcel of land, situate in the COUNTY OF YANKTON and TERRITORY OR DAKOTA, described as follows, to-wit:

Commencing at the North East quarter of Section thirty four (34) Township Ninety six (96) Range Fifty seven (57) Since West of being the middle including (30) townsites. the middle of Concession into Three and Twenty five of as Section Line. thence south along said section line to the Point. Containing about two of one half acre of the said East of said Section the said Thirty four of Hamilton County say of the Range of Township. This Plan of land is compact for Church purpose, and Granted in prosen of said grant the second part as long as it is used for said purpose, continue to end to end by of the said part his their own sim

Together with all and singular the hereditaments and appurtenances thereunto belonging or in anywise appertaining; _____

To Have and to Hold The said premises with the appurtenances to the said part_ies_ of the second part, _____ forever; and the said _Michael Sess and Katharina Sess his wife_ _____ for _himself_ and _their_ heirs, executors and administrators, do _covenant and agree_ to and with the said part_y_ of the second part _____ well seized in fee of the lands and premises aforesaid, and ha_s_ good right and lawful authority to sell and convey the same in manner and form aforesaid; and that the same are free from all incumbrances whatsoever,

And further, that the said part *ies* of the first part for *themselves* ____ and *their* heirs and all and every other person lawfully claiming or to claim by, from or under him, or them, shall and will from time to time, and at all times hereafter, make and execute, or cause and procure to be made and executed, all such further deed or devis whatsoever, for the further and more perfect assurance and confirmation of the said premises hereby granted, with the appurtenances, unto the said part *y* of the second part ____ as by him or them shall be required; and the above granted premises in the quiet and peaceable possession of the said part *y* of the second part ____ ____ heirs, executors and administrators, will WARRANT AND FOREVER DEFEND.

In Witness Whereof, The said part *ies* of the first part ha *s* hereunto set *their* hand *s* and seal *s* the day and year first above written.

Signed and Delivered in Presence of

A. S. Denning   Michael Serr ____ SEAL

O. H. Engel   Katharina Serr ____ SEAL

____ SEAL

____ SEAL

TERRITORY OF DAKOTA, County of Hutchinson, ss.

Be it Remembered, That on this *sixth* day of *February* in the Year One Thousand Eight Hundred and *Eighty-Eight* before me A. S. Denning *Justice of the Peace* within and for said County and Territory, personally appeared Michael Serr and Katharina Serr ____ well known to me to be the person *s* who *are* described in and who executed the within and foregoing instrument, and severally duly acknowledged to me that *they* executed the same freely.

In Witness Whereof, I have hereunto set my hand and official seal at said County, the day and year first above written.

A. S. Denning,
Justice of the Peace ____ A. D. 1888, at 9

I CERTIFY the within instrument was filed for record the 29 day of *February* ____ A. D. 1888, at 9 o'clock ____ minutes A. M., and Recorded in Book 12, page 142, of Warranty Deed Records.

Warranty Deed Record of Michael and Katharina Serr. They donated land for the Hoffnung Reformed Church.

Michael Serr and Katharina Engel Serr. Photo taken in Dakota Territory. Photo courtesy of Jay Keithahn.

According to his death certificate, Michael died 10 July 1919 of old age. Katharina's death certificate states that she died 30 December 1916 from a cerebral hemorrhage and exhaustion. They are both buried in the Community Union Cemetery in Plevna, Montana.

Michael and **Katharina Engel Serr** had ten children.

1. Henry M. b 8 February 1863, Worms, SR, m Katharina Schatz, d 1940 Eureka, McPherson County, SD
2. Jacob M b 13 December 1864, Gnadenfeld, Odessa, SR, m Christine Liedle 14 July 1889, d 1 January 1940 Eureka, McPherson County, SD

3. Rosina b 5 January 1866, Gnadenfeld, SR, m Jacob Stoller 20 October 1889, d 1956 Spokane, WA
4. John Michael b 30 August 1870, Gnadenfeld, SR
5. Karolina b 30 November 1872, SR, m George Stoller 23 December 1890, d December 1949, Spokane, WA
6. Edward b 14 June 1875, Odessa Township, d 14 February 1876, buried Hoffnung Reformed Cemetery
7. Fredericka b 21 May 1877, Odessa Township, m Michael Henne 16 January 1898, d 19 October 1910, Zeeland, ND
8. Edward b 11 December 1879, Odessa Township, d 9 June 1880, buried Hoffnung Reformed Cemetery
9. Joanna b 2 May 1881, Odessa Township, d 23 February 1885, Odessa Township, buried Hoffnung Reformed Cemetery
10. Robert Emil b 9 February 1887, Odessa Township, m 1906 Pauline Karsten

By 1910 **Wilhelm Muller** owned all of Michael and Katherina Serr's land.

Sieler (Seiler)

Heinrich (Henry) Sieler

Heinrich Sieler was born 3 November 1848 to **(Georg) Adam** and **Magdalena Pfaff Sieler**.[1] The records indicate that Adam Sieler's parents were **George** and **Johanna Krause Sieler**. Stumpp's *The Emigration from Germany to Russia in the Years 1763-1862* show that Sieler family, Georg 34, Frau Johanna 32, and children, Elisabeth 12, Georg 10, and Adam 3, arrived in Freudental from Unterböhringen od. Altenstadt/Geißlingen-Weurttemberg.

The St. Petersburg/Freudental death records state that Johann Georg Adam Sieler died 6 January 1851 in Freudental. He was 70 years, 21 days at the time of death, born in Weurttemberg, and his widow's name was **Johanna Krause**.

Adam and Magdalena Pfaff Sieler married 21 February 1837 in Freudental. The St. Petersburg files for Freudental indicate that Magdalena Pfaff was from Peterstal and Adam was from

---

[1] Odessa Digital Library, St. Petersburg Archives, Freudental Birth Records, 184x (R. Wiseman). http://pixel.cs.vt.edu/library/stpete/freud/link/freu184b.txt.

Freudental.[1] Amelia Weidenbach's genealogical research shows that
Magdalena Pfaff was born in 1819 and left Russia in 1884 aboard
the *Elba* with her daughter and son-in-law Jacob and Katherina
Sieler Giegle. Magdalena died in northern South Dakota.
The St. Petersburg files for Freudental indicate that **(Georg)**
Adam and **Magdalena** had the following children:

1. Catharina Barbara b 19 June 1838, Freudental, d 5 July 1838,
   15 days
2. Georg Philipp b 22 Aug. 1839, Freudental
3. Adam b 7 Sept. 1841, Helenental
4. Johann Jacob b 20 Nov. 1843, Freudental
5. Johann Anton b 4 May 1846, Freudental, d 22 Nov. 1868,
   22 yrs, 6 months, 18 days
6. Heinrich b 3 Nov. 1848, Helenental
7. Catharina Elisabeth b 9 May 1851, Helenental
8. Eva Elisabeth b 24 Sept. 1855, Helenetal
9. Caspar b 16 July 1858, Helenental

Henry Sieler married **Elisabeth Jasmann** 25 September 1869.[2]
Born 13 July 1850 at Worms, Elisabeth Jasmann was the daughter
of **Georg** and his first wife **Elizabeth Weidenbach Jasmann** (see
Georg Jasmann biography).[3]
The Sielers were among the third group of Germans to emigrate
from Russia. They sailed from Germany aboard the vessel *Silesia* on
13 November 1872 where "it took us twenty-one days till we
arrived on the 2nd of December, 1872 in New York. After two days
we proceeded to Sandusky."[4]
Following the winter on Kellys Island, "the new immigrants held
a gathering at which they agreed to send out scouts (Kündschafter)
to look around for land which would suit them as a group. Twelve
men were chosen." Henry Sieler was one of the scouts picked to

[1] Odessa Digital Library, St. Petersburg Archives, Freudental Birth Records, 184x
(R. Wiseman). http://pixel.cs.vt.edu/library/stpete/freud/link/freu184b.txt.

[2] Odessa Digital Library, St. Petersburg Archives, Rohrbach Marriage Records,
186x (D. Wahl). http://pixel.cs.vt.edu/library/stpete/rohr/link/rohr186m.txt.

[3] Odessa Digital Library, St. Petersburg Archives, Rohrbach Birth Records, 185x
(D. Wahl). http://pixel.cs.vt.edu/library/stpete/rohr/link/rohr185b.txt.

[4] Rath, p. 64.

search for enough land to live on for their immediate parties and the ones who would still be coming from Russia. After traveling to Michigan, Illinois, Wisconsin, Missouri, Kansas, and Arkansas, six of the scouts returned to Ohio. The remaining six, including Henry Sieler, investigated reports of land in Minnesota, Iowa, and Nebraska. They found what they were looking for in Dakota Territory: "The land, a steppe, similar to the one in Russia."[1]

Henry homesteaded on the northern half of section 30 and the northeast quarter of section 25 in Scotland Township, Bon Homme County, Dakota Territory.

By 1879 the family had moved to Scotland, Bon Homme County, where Sieler owned a grocery and dry goods store.

HENRY SIELER

dealer in

DRY GOODS AND GROCERIES

Notions, Hats, Caps, Boots. Shoes!

I invite an inspection of my goods and prices
for everything is

DOWN!   DOWN!   DOWN.

Corner of Shupe and Curry Streets,
SCOTLAND, D.T.

---

[1] Rath, p. 68.

The following articles appeared in the *Scotland Journal.*

30 August 1888:

> **Henry Sieler's family was enlarged by the arrival of 10 pounds of masculine humanity. Henry Sieler left Monday for Minneapolis, St. Paul and Chicago to buy his fall and winter stock of dry goods.**

18 July 1889:

> **The 4-year-old son of Henry Sieler is a venturesome little fellow. Last Wednesday afternoon he commenced at the low sheds of Max and Baisch's store and climbed to the roof of their store 22 feet high and lost his balance and fell to the ground, and escaped with only a few bruises.**

12 August 1893:

> **Henry Sieler and family and Mrs. Geo. Jasmann and children were passengers to the World's Fair Tuesday.**

Six children of **Henry** and **Elizabeth Sieler's** died in infancy: Elisabeth, Richard, Beata, Henry, Theodore, and Elena. The 1900 U.S. Federal Census shows Henry was 51, married 31 years, born in Russia, his parents were born in Germany, and he came to America in 1872. His wife Elisabeth states that she was 41, married 31 years, the mother of 13 children of which 7 were still living, she and her parents were born in Russia, and she came to America in 1872. They had the following children living at home at the time:

1. Louisa b Oct. 1880
2. George b Oct. 1882
3. Manuel b. Nov. 1884
4. Herbert b Aug. 1888
5. Rosa b April 1890
6. Victor b Feb. 1893
7. Sigamund b July (?) 1895

Around 1908 the Sielers moved to Spokane, Washington. **Elisabeth Jasmann Sieler** died 14 January 1914 in Spokane, Washington, at the age of 63 years 5 months and 15 days. She was survived by her husband, five sons, one daughter, and three brothers—David, Friedrich, and Heinrich Jasmann.[1]

Peter Sieler

Peter Sieler was 19 when he came to America with his older brother **Heinrich Sieler** and his family (see Heinrich Sieler information). They left Helenental, South Russia, boarded a train at Odessa, Russia, and on 13 November 1872, sailed to America on the steamship *Silesia*.

Peter Sieler settled on the northwest quarter, and the southern half of section 19 in Odessa Township. Later he bought land in Bon Homme County and became a successful and influential farmer. The following articles appeared in *The Scotland Journal*.

23 March 1895:

The Wanderer Returns
Peter Seiler who had been a prosperous farmer in this county for the past twenty years became dissatisfied last fall, sold his place and moved his family and household goods to Virginia. Later it began to be talked around that Peter didn't like Virginia as well as he thought he did and finally about a month ago it was reported that he was coming back to Dakota. He said there was advantages in Virginia that we did not have here and at first he thought it was just the place but later on he began to find the defects and finally made up his mind that Dakota was the best after all and concluded to come back. He came here a poor man but by hard work and close attention to business built up quite a fortune.

---

[1] *Heritage Review*, Volume 21, No. 3, September 1991, p.41.

30 March 1895:

> Peter Sieler's car of household goods and stock came in Wednesday from Virginia having been on the road nine days. It seems the car was misdirected some way and went up into Minnesota and from there finally arrived at Scotland all right.

8 February 1896:

> We understand that Peter Seiler has bought a big farm four miles north of Scotland and will take possession in the early spring. Two years ago Peter owned one of the finest farms in this section, but the sourthern fever struck him and he sold out and moved to Virginia, but he didn't stay long. He came back with less money and more knowledge and fortunately still has means enough to start in again in good shape.

19 November 1898:

> Peter Sieler returned from Russia last Wednesday. He brought with him about thirty Russian immigrants who will settle near Tripp in Hutchinson County.

26 November 1898:

> Peter Sieler of Tripp was in town last Wednesday. Peter had just returned from Russia where he went last summer on a visit. When asked what he thought of that country now after living in the United States the past twenty years, he said "I would not live there again if they would give me the best farm in the country."

According to the 1880 U.S. Federal Census for Yankton County, Sieler was 29, a farmer, born in Russia, and his parents were both born in Russia. His wife **Elizabeth** was 24, born in Russia, and both parents were also born in Russia. The two children listed were Julius, 4, and Heinrich, one month. Both children were born in Dakota.

By 1910, **Theodore Ulmer** owned the northwest quarter of section 19. **Gottlieb Ulmer** owned the southwest quarter of section 19. **Christian Mehrer Sr.** owned the southeast quarter of section 19.

Stoller
Heinrich Stoller

Heinrich Stoller was born 8 May 1858 to **Dominik (Dominic)** and **Margaretha Kost Stoller**. Dominik was born circa 1820 in Rohrbach. Margaretha was born circa 1825. Stumpp indicates that Dominik Stoller's family settled in Rohrbach in 1809. Those listed in the Rohrbach "Revisionsliste 1816" in *The Emigration from Germany to Russia in the Years 1763 to 1862* are: Michael 55, seine Frau Magdalena 57, seine Sohne Jakob 21, Christoph, 15 (died in 1814), Dominik 17, Friedrich 15. Another Stoller family is also listed: Andreas 23, seine Frau Magdalena 20, seine Sohne Johann 1½, Ludwig ½.

According to the St. Petersburg records for Rohrbach, Dominik Stoller married **Magdalena Bachman** on 30 November 1843.[1] The Rohrbach files for the 1840's show that the couple appeared to have the following children:

1. Margaretha b 11 March 1845
2. Regina b 16 Nov. 1846
3. Christina b 11 Dec. 1848 d 16 May 1868, 19 yrs, 4 months, 6 days.
4. Katharina b May 1851

Magdalena died 31 December 1852. Dominik then married **Margaretha Kost** on 31 May 1853. **Margaretha** and **Dominik** had the following children:

1. Magdalena b 9 April 1855
2. Dominik b 22 Jan. 1857 d 22 Jan. 1857, 2 hrs.

---

[1] Odessa Digital Library, St. Petersburg Archives, Rohrbach Marriage Records, 184x (D. Wahl). http://pixel.cs.vt.edu/library/stpete/rohr/link/rohr184m.txt.

3. Heinrich b 8 May 1858
4. Elisabetha b April 1860
5. Johannes b 24 June 1862
6. Friedrich b 6 Feb. 1867
7. Georg b 12 May 1869

*Dominic and Margaretha (Kost) Stoller, parents of Heinrich Stoller.
Photo couretesy of Della Kiesz.*

The Stoller family, including fifteen-year-old Heinrich Stoller, went through the expensive and "time-consuming" ordeal of obtaining traveling passports in order to leave Russia. He and his family were part of "the third group which also went to America in the late fall of 1872."[1]

> "But when you came to the provincial office the road at our time for the most part was prepared by bribing lower officials. Once you held the passport, there were no further difficulties to be expected at the state line. Our group consisted of six families. These were: Dominik Stoller, Michael Stoller, George Wind [Mind?], Georg Jasmann, Christian Jasmann, Heinrich Sieler. In addition there were two unmarried boys, H. Sieler from Helenetal and his brother Peter."[2]**

In a letter to George Rath, author of *The Black Sea Germans in the Dakotas*, Stoller stated that after they arrived in Berlin, the party went to Hamburg before sailing to America aboard the *Silesia* "where we had to stay a few days more till our ship set out to sea." Although the trip was supposed to take only fourteen days, storms caused the journey to last twenty-one days. They arrived in New York 2 December 1872, then left for Sandusky in order to meet up with others from Russia.[3]

Heinrich Stoller arrived in Dakota Territory in April 1873 along with the rest of his father's family. The steamship *Silesia* lists the following:

Stoller, Dominic   male   53   years old
    Margarete   fem   48   " "
    Magdalene   f   18   " "
    Heinrich   m   15   " "
    Elizabeth [4]

---

[1] Rath, p. 64.

[2] Ibid.

** According to the ship list, Heinrich Sieler was married, had a family, and Peter Sieler accompanied Heinrich and family to America.

[3] Ibid.

[4] Rath, p. 65.

While Dominik and his family members settled in Jamesville Township, Yankton County, **Heinrich Stoller** applied for naturalization on 9 May 1879 and homesteaded on the northeast quarter of section 17 in Odessa Township. According to *MENNO: The First 100 Years*, Stoller married **Christina Muehlbeier** in 1879.

According to the 1880 census, Heinrich was 22, a farmer, born in Russia, and both parents were born in Russia. His wife Christina (Muehlbeier[1]) was 20, born in Russia, and both of her parents were born in Russia.

The *Scotland Journal* states the following about the Heinrich Stoller family and the hardships he and others endured in Dakota:

> **Diptheria is said to be raging in the German settlement six miles southeast of town. At the home of Henry Stoller, one child is dead and four others are down with the dread disease. Other cases are reported in the neighborhood, but there is only one fatal case so far.**

Margaretha Kost Stoller died in 1899 at the age of 73.

By 1910 **Heinrich Stoller** owned 320 acres, the northern half of section 17 in Odessa Township.

Ulmer
Matthias Ulmer

According to a number of sources, including the 1900 U.S. Federal Census, the 1830 St. Petersburg birth records for Rohrbach, and the *Johannestal Beresan District Odessa 1858 Census*, **Matthias Ulmer** was born 2 November 1835 in Johannestal, South Russia, to **Jakob** and **Christina Brenner Ulmer**. The 1830 marriage records for Rohrbach state that Jakob and Christina were married 15 December 1833.

Around 1858 Matthias married **Catharina Delzer** who was born 26 March 1837 to **Ludwig** and **Sophia Eisinger Delzer**. Ludwig and Sophia were born circa 1816.[2] The death records for Rohrbach

---

[1] *MENNO, p. 579.*

[2] *Johannestal Beresan District Odessa 1858 Census.*

state that **Catharina Ulmer** died in Johannestal, South Russia, on 31 October 1869 when she was 32 years, 6 months, and 5 days.

Matthias then married **Elisabetha Klink Ulmer** on 17 February 1870.[1] Elizabeth was born 31 March 1841 in Johannestal, South Russia, to **Johannes** and **Annette Klink**. Elisabetha had married **Christian Ulmer** on 20 December 1858. He died in 1866. From this union came four children. **Matthias** and **Elisabetha's** marriage produced eight children.[2]

Matthias Ulmer and family left Johannestal, South Russia, and came to America aboard the vessel Schiller on 20 August 1874. Along with Matthias 37, and Elizabeth 34, the following children also came: Andreas 18, Catherine 15, Gottlieb 14, Wilhelm 9, Carolina 10, Maria 8, Christian 7, Jacob 5, Fredericka 11/12, and Carl 1/12.[3]

Ulmer homesteaded on the northwest quarter, the northeast quarter and the southeast quarters of section 1 in Odessa Township. He received his naturalization papers in 1879.

The 1880 U.S. Federal Census states the following about **Matthias** and **Elizabeth Ulmer**: Matthias was 45, born in Russia, his mother and father were born in Wuerttemberg; Elizabeth was 39, born in Russia, her father was born in Wuerttemberg, and her mother was born in Russia.

The same census lists the following children:

1. Wilhelm 19	6. Frederika 8
2. Carolina 19	7. Carl 7
3. Maria 17	8. Louisa 4
4. Christian 15	9. Johannes 1
5. Jakob 11	

In 1903 **Ulmer** moved to Menno, South Dakota, where he died 26 January 1906 at the age of 70 years 2 months and 20 days.[4] **Elizabeth** died 12 June 1914, also at Menno.[5]

---

[1] Odessa Digital Library, St. Petersburg Archives, Rohrbach Marriage Records, 187x (D. Wahl). http://pixel.cs.vt.edu/library/stpete/rohr/link/rohr187m.txt.

[2] *Heritage Review*, Volume 21, No. 3, September 1991, 386, 43.

[3] Pritzkau, p. 63.

[4] *Heritage Review*, September 1989, pp. 58, 23.

[5] *Heritage Review*, September 1991, p. 43.

By 1910 the original homestead land that took up the northern half of section 1 was owned by **Emanuel Ulmer**, and **Johannes Ulmer** owned the southeastern quarter.

Vaatz
August Vaatz

August Vaatz homesteaded on the western half of section 27 in Odessa Township.

By 1910 **Frederick Frank** owned the northwestern quarter of section 27 and **Heinrich Stoller** owned the southwestern quarter of section 27.

Weber
Konrad Weber

Konrad Weber's homestead land consisted of most of the northern half of section 6. He was born in 1854 and came to America in 1875. He applied for naturalization on 22 May 1876. By 1910 the Hutterite Brethren Colony owned his original homestead land and he was living in Township 97 of Hutchinson County with a **Carolina** and **Doretha Weber**.

Weidenbach
Heinrich Weidenbach

Amelia Weidenbach found in her family research that the tie to the Weidenbach family name, meaning "willow brook," goes back to 1096 to a crusader from Thuringen. The Weidenbach coat-of-arms shows six willow leaves in green on silver and six in silver on green.

The family records show the descendants of **Johann Konrad Weidenbach** and **Philippine Muhlhauser** lived in the village of Albersweiler, Pfalz, Germany (the Palatinate). According to the Albersweiler Reformed Church records, on 4 March 1767 a son named Johann Konrad was born. **Johann Konrad** married **Eva Katharina Michel**. They had the following children:

1. George Heinrich b 3 August 1799 in Alberseiler, Germany
2. Maria Katharina b 18 August 1802 in Alberseiler, Germany
3. Sibylla b 12 March 1805 in Alberseiler, Germany
4. Eva Katharina b 29 June 1807 in Alberseiler, Germany
5. Kasper b circa 1810 in Worms, Russia

Georg Heinrich, or Heinrich as he was called later, migrated to Worms, Russia, when he was between 9 and 10 (the 1858 census records for Worms states that the family arrived in 1809). He was confirmed in 1814. Later he married **Anna Margaretta Kussler**. She died 13 September 1864 in Russia. Their known children were:

1. Konrad b 27 April 1820
2. Elizabeth b 1 February 1829, m 12 November 1846 Georg Fredrich Jasmann[1]
3. Margareth b 14 May 1830[2] d 8 Dec. 1838[3]
4. Catherine b 30 Dec. 1836[4] d 1 Sept. 1838[5]
5. Heinrich b 16 September 1840[6]

On 11 December 1857, **Heinrich**, Georg Heinrich's son, married **Friederika Jungmann** in Worms, Russia. Friederika was born 15 May 1838.

Heinrich Sr. remarried. St. Petersburg records indicate that he married **Elisabeth Schoeck** on 17 January 1865 in Johannesthal.[7] **Elisabeth's [Billigmeier]** first husband could be **Georg Heinrich Schoeck** whom she married 30 May 1833 in Rohrbach. The 1830

---

[1] Odessa Digital Library, St. Petersburg Archives, Rohrbach Marriage Records, 184x (D. Wahl). http://pixel.cs.vt.edu/library/stpete/rohr/link/rohr184m.txt.

[2] Odessa Digital Library, St. Petersburg Archives, Rohrbach Birth Records, 183x (D. Wahl). http://pixel.cs.vt.edu/library/stpete/rohr/link/rohr183b.txt.

[3] Odessa Digital Library, St. Petersburg Archives, Rohrbach Death Records, 183x (D. Wahl). http://pixel.cs.vt.edu/library/stpete/rohr/link/rohr183d.txt.

[4] Odessa Digital Library, St. Petersburg Archives, Rohrbach Birth Records, 183x (D. Wahl). http://pixel.cs.vt.edu/library/stpete/rohr/link/rohr183b.txt.

[5] Odessa Digital Library, St. Petersburg Archives, Rohrbach Death Records, 185x (D. Wahl). http://pixel.cs.vt.edu/library/stpete/rohr/link/rohr185d.txt.

[6] Odessa Digital Library, St. Petersburg Archives, Rohrbach Death Records, 186x (D. Wahl). http://pixel.cs.vt.edu/library/stpete/rohr/link/rohr186d.txt.

[7] Odessa Digital Library, St. Petersburg Archives, Rohrbach Marriage Records, 186x (D. Wahl). http://pixel.cs.vt.edu/library/stpete/rohr/link/rohr186m.txt.

Rohrbach marriage files state that Elisabetha was 19 years old and the daughter of **Jakob** and **Catharina Kranzbuchler** of Waterloo. **Georg Heinrich Schoeck** was 20 and the son of **Ernst** and **Maria Pfuester** of Waterloo.

The ship list for the steamship *Thuringia* lists the following Weidenbach family members to arrive at New York on 30 July 1873:

Heinrich	33	M	Farmer
Friedricke	33	F	wife
Hein.	8	M	children
Wilh.	6	M	"
Elisa.	14	F	"
Marie	9	F	"
Cath.	8	F	"
Heh.	70	M	farmer
Elisa.	60	F	wife [1]

Heinrich Weidenbach Jr. and Heinrich Weidenbach Sr. homesteaded on the southern half of section 20. Heinrich Weidenbach Jr. later bought the southwest quarter of section 21 from **Georg Jasmann** for $400[2] where "[A] sod house was built on the original homestead. Wheat was the main crop, with oats and hay, with pasture for the horses and cattle."[3] The original homestead map states that Weidenbach also claimed the southeast quarter of section 33. He helped organize the German Reformed Odessa Church that was located on section 31. Heinrich also donated one acre of land in section 20 to the Odessa School District #24.[4]

Eugene Weidenbach, another Odessa historian, tells about his ancestors. He states that shortly after the Weidenbachs arrived in Odessa Township, Friederika became homesick. She told her husband that she wished that she had "but one hen that would lay an egg once in a while."

---

[1] *Heritage Review*, North Dakota Historical Society of Germans from Russia, Bismarck, North Dakota, Volumes 5 and 6, June 1973, p. 44.

[2] *Yankton County History*, Yankton County Historical Society, Yankton, South Dakota, and Curtis Media Corporation, Dallas, Texas, 1987, p. 700.

[3] Ibid.

[4] *Yankton County History*, Yankton County Historical Society, Yankton, South Dakota, and Curtis Media Corporation, Dallas, Texas, 1987, p. 700.

Heinrich promised her that as soon as he got the crop in he would take her to visit his brother Konrad and his wife Christina who only lived about five miles away. Maybe, he told her, they could give her a hen. After the crop was in, they visited Heinrich's brother and sister-in-law who gave Friederika two hens and a rooster. From this she hatched twenty-seven chicks.

The church records show the following children belonging to **Heinrich** and **Friederika Weidenbach**:

1. Elisabeth b 17 May 1859, Worms, SR, confirmed 1873, m 22 October 1878 Peter Zeeb (b 20 December 1854 Friedenstal, Heilborn, Crimea, Russia). (Amelia Weidenbach claims that with Wilhelm Mueller, Zeeb arrived aboard the ship *Lessing* on 3 July 1874. He homesteaded the SW quarter of section 27 in Sweet Township, Hutchinson County, and was an elder in the Menno Reformed Church.) Elizabeth d 29 July 1943, buried Menno Cemetery, Menno, SD. Peter, d 26 January 1922, buried Menno Cemetery, Menno, SD.

2. Catharina b 26 June 1863, Worms, SR, confirmed 13 February 1876, m 1885 Frederich Goehring (b 1 February 1862 Kassel, Russia). Goehring was a furniture dealer and mortician with a funeral parlor in Scotland, SD. Catharina d 21 January 1936, buried Rosehill Cemetery, Scotland, SD

3. Frederich, d 10 May 1944, buried Rosehill Cemetery, Scotland, SD

4. Heinrich b 7 November 1864, Worms, SR, confirmed 30 May 1880, m 19 February 1888 Elizabeth Hieb (b 22 November 1870). Heinrich d 13 February 1933, buried Rosehill Cemetery, Scotland, SD. Elizabeth d 2 October 1943, buried Rosehill Cemetery, Scotland, SD

5. Wilhelm b 16 November 1869, Worms, SR, confirmed 30 May 1884, m 1896 Elisabeth Barth (b November 1876, Wilhelm, d 1933, Hettinger, ND)

6. Christina b 25 November 1876, Dakota Territory, m Gottlieb Hertz April 1899. Christina d 16 November 1948, buried Rosehill Cemetery, Scotland, SD. Gottlieb d 1 May 1945, buried Rosehill Cemetery, Scotland, SD

7. Friederika b 21 May 1878, Yankton, DT m Jacob Brosz 19 May 1910

8. Wilhelmina b 19 January 1880m Yankton, DT, m Wilhelm Knodt. Wilhelmina d 1958 bur Hartford, SD
9. Lydia b 14 August 1882 m 7 Jan. 1905 Christian Bertsch. Lydia d 14 Jan 1958 Menno.

[Georg] **Heinrich Weidenbach Sr.**'s wife **Elisabeth** died before the 1880 U.S. Federal Census and he died sometime after. Amelia Weidenbach says the family assumes he is buried in the German Reformed Odessa Church Cemetery.
Heinrich Weidenbach Jr. died 16 November 1924 at Scotland, South Dakota. **Friederika Jungmann Weidenbach** died 18 January 1908. They are both buried in the Rosehill Cemetery at Scotland, South Dakota.

Werner
David Werner

The 1840 St. Petersburg birth records for Rohrbach indicate that **David Werner** was born October 1841 **Johannes** and **Barbara Stauss Werner** of Worms. Besides David, the 1830 birth records indicate the Werners had the following children:

1. Johanna (Ana) (twin) b 14 Jan. 1834 d 18 Nov. 1835, 1 ¾ yrs
2. Katharina (twin) b 14 Jan. 1834 d 26 Nov. 1835, 1¾ yrs.
3. Maria Elisabeth b 20 Feb. 1836
4. Anton b 3 Dec. 1837
5. Margaretha b 13 Nov. 1839 d Feb. 1842, 2 yrs. 3 mo.

The 1840 Rohrbach death records indicate that Johannes Werner was born in Kirschdorf and died March 1841 when he was 37. On 20 February 1845, **Barbara Stauss Werner** married **Konrad Reiser**.[1] The *Worms, Beresan District Odessa, 1858 Census* states that Konrad died in 1852 and son Christoph died in 1850.

David Werner homesteaded on part of the southern half of section 25. According to the 1880 U.S. Federal Census, Werner was 38, a farmer, and born in Russia. His father was born in Prussia, and his mother was born in Baden. His wife **Phillipina** was 36 and born in Russia. Her father was born in Wuerttemberg; her mother was born in Russia. They had the following children living with them at the time:

1. Wilhelm 13
2. Friederick 10
3. Christina 6
4. Jakob 5/12

By 1910 **Lars A. Bruce** owned the original tract that Werner once homesteaded.

---

[1] Odessa Digital Library, St. Petersburg Archives, Rohrbach Marriage Records, 184x (D. Wahl). http://pixel.cs.vt.edu/library/stpete/rohr/link/rohr184m.txt.

Winter
Wilhelmina Winter

Wilhelmina Schulz Winter came to America with her husband **Simon Winter** in 1874. Wilhelmina Schulz was born 11 July 1852 to **Daniel** and **Anna Dorothea Schulz** in Dennewitz, Bessarabia.[1] Records indicate **Johann Schulz, Wilhelmina Tiede**, and **Wilhelmina Schulz** were her godparents.[2] The 1900 U.S. Federal Census for Hutchinson County states Daniel was born June 1823 and Anna Dorothea was born June 1831. With their children, the Schulzes settled in Township 97 of Range 57 of Hutchinson County in 1874. The records also state that Anna Dorothea had 14 children of which 5 were still living.

Simon's parents were **Daniel** and **Marie Jarcho Winter** who were married 5 October 1838 in Tarutino, Bessarabia. Yankton County Naturalization records indicate that Daniel was born in 1820. The 1880 U.S. Federal Census shows that Marie was born in June 1822. Simon was born 6 September 1841 in Kassel.[3] He and Wilhelmina were married 23 May 1871 at Benkendorf, Bessarabia.[4] Wilhelmina's homestead or tree claim land in Odessa Township took up the northeast quarter of section 19. Simon and Wilhelmina also had land on sections 18 and 19 in Sweet Township, Hutchinson County.

The 1880 U.S. Federal Census for Township 97 of Range 57 in Hutchinson County states that **Simon** was 38, **Wilhelmina** was 27, and they had the following children (the information in parentheses reflects the 1900 U.S. Census for Hutchinson County):

1. Robert 8 (b Aug. 1872)
2. Rebecka 5 (b Aug. 1874)
3. Henride 4 (Henriette b May 1876)
4. Louisa 2
5. Mathilda 1

[1] *MENNO*, pp. 603-604.
[2] Odessa Digital Library, St. Petersburg Archives, Bessarabian Village Birth Recs, 185x (R. Drefs). http://pixel.cs.vt.edu/library/stpete/bess/link/bes185xb.txt.
[3] Odessa Digital Library, St. Petersburg Archives, Glueckstal Birth Recs, 184x (D. Wahl). http://pixel.cs.vt.edu/library/stpete/gluc/link/glueckbm.txt.
[4] Odessa Digital Library, St. Petersburg Archives, Bessarabian Village Marr Recs, 187x (R. Drefs) http://pixel.cs.vt.edu/library/stpete/bess/link/bess187m.txt.

The Winters also had the following children. Some of these children are listed in the 1900 U.S. Federal Census:

6. Edward 15 b May 1885
7. William 16 b Oct. 1883
8. Rudolph 12 b May 1888
9. Arthur 6 b June 1893
10. Matilda
11. Dorethea 18 (Dora b Aug. 1881)[1]

According to the Hutchinson County Cemetery list, **Wilhelmina** died when she was 65 and **Simon** died when he was 79. They are both buried in the cemetery in Menno, South Dakota.

Ziegele
Carl Ziegele

Information found in the St. Petersburg birth records for 1840 and 1850, and the *Waterloo, Beresan District Odessa, 1858 Census* shows that **Carl Ziegele** was born 29 August 1846 in Gnadenfeld, South Russia, to **Johann** and **Elisabetha Brenneisen (Breneisse, Breneise)**. The records also indicate that Johann and Elisabetha Ziegele had the following children:

1. Johann b ~ 1831 m Magdalena Speh 22 Sept. 1853, Rohrbach
2. Philipp b ~ 1833 m Carolina Schiermeister, Rohrbach and Paris
3. Katharina Barbara b 20 Sept. 1833
4. Sophia b 10 Dec. 1836
5. Rosina b 29 Jan. 1838
6. Friederika b 7 Aug. 1839
7. Elisabetha b 20 Jan. 1841
8. Gottlieb b 22 Sept. 1842 d 8 Dec. 1842, 2 yrs old
9. Michael b 14 Feb. 1844 m Friederika Klein[2]
10. infant b 17 Sept. 1845 (stillborn)
11. Carl b 29 Aug. 1846
12. Margaretha b 3 July 1851

---

[1] *MENNO*, pp. 603-604.

[2] Odessa Digital Library, St. Petersburg Archives, Rohrbach Birth Records, 187x (D. Wahl). http://pixel.cs.vt.edu/library/stpete/rohr/link/rohr187b.txt.

13. Wilhelm b 5 March 1853
14. Peter b 12 May 1855 d 11 July 1858

The *Waterloo, Beresan District Odessa, 1858 Census* shows that **Johann Ziegele Jr.** was 49 and **Elisabetha** was 50. His father **Johann Ziegele Sr.** was 75 and arrived in the Caucasus in 1817 from Reichenbach, Esslingen, Wuerttemberg. The elder Ziegele's wife **Saroara** (the 1850 Rohrbach death records show his wife to be **Rosina**) died 24 October 1852 at the age of 78 years, 6 months, and 24 days. The 1860 Rohrbach death records show Johann Ziegele Sr. died 16 July 1868 in Waterloo at the age of 85 years, 4 months, and 29 days. The 1870 Rohrbach death records also state that Johann Ziegele Jr. was born in Reichenberg and he died 27 August 1876 at the age of 64 years 2 months 28 days.

Carl Ziegele married **Marie Engel**, daughter of **Johann** and **Elizabeth Berndt Engel**, who was born 11 March 1847 in Neu-Danzig, South Russia.

In 1873 Carl 27, Marie 26, and Frederick 2 sailed to America aboard the *Westphalia*. Marie's parents, her two brothers, and her brother-inlaw and sister, **Michael** and **Catherina Engel Serr**, and their family arrived at the Port of New York the same day in July 1873 aboard the same ship (see Engel biographies).

Carl Ziegele applied for naturalization on 31 July 1873. He homesteaded on the central, south, and western portions of section 24 and a small part of the northwest quarter of section 25 of Odessa Township. He helped organize the Hoffnung Reformed Church.

The following is a list of the Ziegele children:

1. Frederick b 27 November 1870, Russia, m ____ Schatz
2. Alexander b 28 February 1872
3. Sophia b 3 May 1874, Odessa Township, DT, d 28 August 1894, buried Hoffnung Reformed Cemetery, DT
4. Edward b 25 August 1875, Odessa Township, DT, d 25 August 1894, buried Hoffnung Reformed Cemetery
5. Emil b 2 August 1877, Odessa Township, DT
6. Emanuel b 13 November 1877, Odessa Township, DT
7. Carl b 7 October 1881, Odessa Township, DT, d 23 July 1893, buried Hoffnung Reformed Cemetery

8. Johanna b 20 March 1883, Odessa Township, d 13 July 1893, buried Hoffnung Reformed Cemetery
9. Rosina b 15 December 1884, Odessa Township, d 5 July 1893, buried Hoffnung Reformed Cemetery
10. Karolina b 15 September 1886, Odessa Township, d 7 July 1893, buried Hoffnung Reformed Cemetery
11. Julia b 6 July 1888, Odessa Township, d 23 June 1893, buried Hoffnung Reformed Cemetery

Sometime around 1895, the Ziegele family moved to Portland, Oregon, where Carl worked in a shoe repair shop. The following article was found in the 30 November 1895 issue of the the *Scotland Journal* concerning Ziegele's potential move to Oregon:

> **Carl Ziegle [sic] and family, George Stowler [sic] and John Serr, and the family of Henry Serr and Miss Rosa Wisser, of Tyndall left Wednesday for Yankton, where they will take a special car over the Great Northern railway for Oregon, where they expect to reside.**

By 1910 Ziegele's homestead land was owned by **Jacob M. Diede**.

Bibliography

Daily Press and Dakotan (The), Yankton, Dakota Territory. 1878.

Dakota Citizen (The), Hutchinson County, Dakota Territory. 1884.

Die Deutsche Auswanderung Nach Russland 1763-1862 (E. Wise)
Published by the Odessa Digital Library - 2 May 1999
http://pixel.cs.vt.edu/library/odessa.html

Gulling, Ken. Letters to author. 1993-2002.

Heritage Review. Germans from Russia Heritage Society. Bismarck,
North Dakota. 1973-1995.

History of Yankton County. The Yankton County Historical Society,
Yankton, South Dakota, and Curtis Media Corporation, Dallas,
Texas. 1987.

Kiesz, Della. Letters to author. 1993-2002.

Kingsbury, George. *History of Dakota Territory*. S.J. Clarke
Publishing Company, Chicago. 1915.

Kusler, Walter. *The Kuslers and Their Descendants*. Self-published.
1983.

Menno Historical Research Committee. *MENNO: The First 100
Years. Freeman South Dakota:* Pine Hill Press. 1979.

Odessa Group (Odessa Digital Library). Odessa: A German-Russian
Genealogical Library. http://pixel.cs.vt.edu.library.odessa.html.

Odessa Township Homestead Map of Yankton County. 1989.
County Atlas Company, P.O. Box 1452, Watertown, SD, 57201.
(605) 882-4196.

Pritzkau, Gwen. "Passenger Lists." Work Paper #12, August, 1973. Lincoln, Nebraska: American Historical Society of Germans from Russia.

Rath, George. *The Black Sea Germans in the Dakotas.* Freeman, South Dakota: Pine Hill Press. 1977.

Renz, Curt. Letters to Author. 1993-2002.

Rothery, Deborah. Letters to author. 1993-1996.

Sallet, Richard. *Russian-German Settlements in the United States.* North Dakota Institute for Regional Studies. 1974.

Scotland Journal (The). Scotland, South Dakota. 1895, 1896, 1911.

Stumpp, Karl. *The Emigration From Germany to Russia in the Years 1763-1862.* Lincoln, Nebraska: American Historical Society of Germans from Russia. 1982.

Wagner, Sally Roesch. *Daughters of Dakota: Schooled in Privation.* Yankton, South Dakota: 1991.

Weidenbach, Amelia. Letters to author. 1991-2002.

Weidenbach, Eugene. Interview. 1995.

FULLNAME INDEX

DELZER (cont.)
  Karolina 75 Katharina 2
  Ludwig 112 Sophia Eisinger
  112
DIEDE, (Anna) Marie Diede 82
  Anna Christina 48 83 Anna
  Christine 83 Anna Margarethe
  Muller 82 Anna Maria 83
  Carolina 83 Catharina 48-49 83
  Christian 49 83 Gottlieb 48-49
  82-83 Heinrich 83 Jacob 49
  Jacob M 6 123 Johann Christian
  49 Johann Gottlieb 83 Johann
  Jacob 83 Margaretha 83 Maria
  Dorothea 83 Meta 95 Michael
  49 83 Michael (1) 48 Michael
  (2) 48 Regine 83 Rosine 83
DIETRICH, Justina 64
DREFS, Helena 8
DUX, August 6 Henrietha
  Wendschlaag 6 Michael 6
EDINGER, Rosina 19
EISSINGER, Catarina 84 Johannes
  84 Magdalena 84
ENGEL, Alvin 9 August 9
  Augustus Wilhelm 8 Barbara 8
  34 Bertha 9 Carolina 8 Carolina
  Suess 9 Catherina 122 Edward
  9 Elizabeth 8 42 67 Elizabeth
  Berndt 6 9 13 34 67 96 122
  Emil Robert 8 Emma 8 Etna E
  9 Fredericka 8 Friedericka 67
  Helena 8 Jacob 8 Johann 6 9 13
  34 42 67 96 122 Johann George
  6 Johanna 8 42 Johanna Rose 9
  Johannes George 8-10 John 10
  John G 9 Julius 9 Katharina 67
  96 Katherina 8 Lydia 9 Marie 8
  122 Martha 9 Philip 8 26 Phillip
  9 Rosina 6 8 13 32 Sarah 9
  Violet 9
ENGLE, Emma 65 Theodore 65
FISCHER, Ida 65

FRANK, Albert 18 28 Amelia 12
  Andreas 12-13 26 29 32 82
  Andreas (Andrew) 10 Anna 29
  Anna Maria 18 Annie 27 Bertha
  12 28-29 Carolina 18 Caroline
  28 Catharina 29 32 Catharina
  Koschel 32 Christ 12 Christian
  28 Christina 26 32 38 Christina
  Horst 27 Elisabethe 32
  Elizabeth 13 18 28 32 Elizabeth
  Theurer 27 Ella 28 Emil 12
  Emmanuel 12 Eva Margaretha
  78 Fred 25 Frederich Jr 18 25
  Frederick 114 Fredreck 18
  Friederich 26 Friedrich 8 13-21
  25-26 29 32 34 82 Friedrich Sr
  13 Friedrick 22-23 George 25
  Gottlieb 10 13 26 30-32
  Gottlieb (1) 28 Gottlieb (2) 28-
  29 Gottlieb Christian 29
  Gottlieb Jr 26-29 32 38 Gottlieb
  Sr 22-24 28-29 Helena 12 18
  Henry 27 Herbert 28 Herbert
  Emil 28 Ida M 28 Jacob 32 78
  Jacob Heinrich 28 Jacobina 12
  Johann Georg 32 Johann
  George 12 18 Johanna 26
  Juliana 78 Julius 28 Katharina
  28 32 Katherina Koschel 10 13
  26 Laura 12 Lea Magdalena 28
  Louisa 19 25-26 Louisa Berndt
  21 Louisa Berndt Boettcher 20
  Lydia Maria Magdalena 12
  Magdalena 10 12-13 32
  Magdalena Freier 12 Maria
  Magdalena 29 Martha 28 Mrs
  Andrew 13 Paulina 18 Pauline
  12 Peter 32 Philip 12 Richard
  12 Rosa 25 Rosina 8 18-19 25
  29 32 34 Rosina Engel 13 34
  Salomine 12 Solomon 19 25
  Theodore 12 Theophiel (Taft)
  28 Wilhelm 14 25 29 32

HERTZ, Christina 117 Gottlieb
117 Otilla 89
HERZ, Katharina 28
HERZEL, Christina 2
HETZLER, Mary 52
HOEFFLE, Bertha 29
HOFFMAN, Jakobine 78
HOLT, Christiana 95 Frank 95
HORST, (Jakob) Friedrich 37 Anna
Maria (Barbara) 37 Barbara
Bengert 37 Catharina Salomea
37 Catharine 37 Catherine 38
Christina 26 32 38 Frederich 38
Friedrich 37-38 Georg 37 Jacob
38 Jakob 37-38 Johann 3 26 37-
39 Katharina 37 Katharine 38
Katharine Muehlbeier 26
Louisa 38 Ludwig 37
Margareth 38 Margretha 38
Maria 37
ISAAK, John 19
JANDA, Joseph 41
JASMAN, Christian 71 Dave 42
George 71 Rosa 56
JASMANN, (Georg) Heinrich 54
56 (Henrika) Henrietta 56 Adolf
44 Agatha 44 Alexander 53
Amalia 40 Anna 45 Anton 55-
56 C 41 Catharina 39 49 51
Catharina Barbara Muller Diede
Kussler 75 Catharina Muller
Diede Kussler 49 59 Catharine
Muller 52 Catherine 40
Christian 39-41 45 49 51 72
111 Christina 45 Christine 45
Clara 53 David 46 49 51-52 107
Doris 56 Edward G 53
Elisabeth 39 104 Elizabeth 44
51 54 115 Elizabeth
Weidenbach 46 104 Elizabetha
45 Elsie (Eliza) 40 Emilie 40
Emma 39 40 Ernest 53 Eva 55
Eva Fercho 44 Frederick 49

JASMANN (cont.)
Fredrich G 52 Friedrich 49 55-
56 107 Georg 46-47 49 104 111
116 Georg F 51 Georg Fredrich
Sr 42 44 54 Georg Friedrich 48
51-52 55 Georg Friedrich Sr 49
Georg Jr 42-43 49 Georg Sr 44
50-51 George 8 43 45 51 72
George Edward 53 George
Fredrich 115 George Fredrick
45 George H 44 George Jr 39
George Sr 39 Gertrude 53
Heinrich 46 48-49 54-55 107
Heinrich George 55 Henrietta
55 Henry 51 Henry Georg(e) 53
Herbert Albert 55 Herman H 53
Hugo 53 Ida A 52 Jakob 45
Jennie 44 Johann 45 55 Johann
Georg 44 Johanna 8 42 Johanna
Engel 43 Johanna (Schindler)
45 Johanna Rosine 44 Julia 55
Juliana 40 Juliane 40 Julie 39
Karl 45 Katharina 45 50
Katherina 42 Lillie 56 Lydia 42
44 Magdalena 46 48 Magdalena
Mitzel Wagner Hauck 47
Magdalina Mitzel Wagner
Hauck 53 Mary 52-53 Mary
Hetzler 52 Maximillian 53
Minnie 53 55 Mrs Geo 106
Norine 53 Otto 53 55 Paul 45
Pauline 55-56 Philip 45 Phillip
45 54-57 Phillip Jr 56 Robert 40
Roland 52 Rosina 49 52 54-57
Rosina (Rosa) 53 Rosina
Schindler 54 Rosine 46 Rudolf
55 Ruth 53 Waldamor Theodor
55 Walter 55 Wilhelm 55-57
Wilhelmina 40 William 55
JASSMAN, Catherine 45-46
Elizabeth 45 Frederick 46 Geo
42-43 George 42 George
Friedrich 46 Magdalena 46

JASSMANN, Georg Friedrich Sr
45 George 8 Johanna 8 Philip
56
JUNGMAN, Emil 95 Margret 95
JUNGMANN, Friederika 115
Nikolaus 33
KARSTEN, Pauline 103
KAUTZ, Christina Schaefer
Kussler 66 Martha 66 Michael
66
KEITHAHN, Jay 102
KIESZ, Della 58 110
KLEIN, Dorothea 19 Friederika
121
KLINK, Annette 113 Johannes 113
KLUCK, Andrew 19 Katherine 19
KNODEL, Elizabeth 4
KNODT, Wilhelm 118 Wilhelmina
118
KOCH, Rosina 8
KOSCHEL, (Anna) Maria Agnesia
29 Catharina 29 Jacob 29
KOST, (Johann) Jakob 57 Anna
Maria 58 Carl 57 Catharina 58
Christian 58 Christine 57 David
57-58 Frederick 57 Jacob 57-58
Jakob 16 57 Johanna (Hanna)
96 Karl 58 Louisa 57 Margareth
69 Margaretha 109 Margaretha
Lutz 57-58 Peter 58 Philipp 58
KOTH, Amalia 37 John 37
KRANZBUCHLER, Catharina 116
Elisabetha 116
KRAUSE, Johanna 103
KUCH, Christ 55 Julia 55
KUSLER, 58 Adam 64 August 64
Catharina 62 Christina 62 86
Christine 64 Elisabeth 64
Elizabeth 64 Gottlieb 64
Heinrich 62 Henry 61 64 Jacob
3 61-63 Johann 62 John 64
Katharina 62 Katherina
Schaeffer 62 Katherine 64

KUSLER (cont.)
Magdalena 64 Martha 64 Mrs
61 Regina 64 75 Rosina Schafer
Auch 3 Sophia 62 Walter M 63
William 64
KUSSLER, (Eva) Catharina
Schaefer 59 Adam 59 Anna
Margaretta 46 115 Carolina 65
Catharina 59 Catharina Barbara
Muller (Mueller) Diede 48
Catharina Diede 49 Catharina
Muller Diede 59 Christiana 64-
65 Christina 63 Christina
Schaefer 66 Christina Schaeffer
62 Elisabeth 58-59 Elizabeth 59
64-65 Elizabeth Munsch 58
Elizabetha 62 Emanuel 65
Emma 65 Georg 59 Heinrich 59
Henry 65 Ida 65 Jacob 58-59 61
64 Jakob 60 Johann 59-60 62-
64 75 Johann Sr 62 Johannes 49
58-59 John L 65 John Sr 63
Louisa 59 65 Ludwig 61 64-66
Magdalena 65 Margaretha 59
Regina 59 65 Rosina Schaeffer
Auch 62
LEUSI, Wilhelmina 87 89
LIBAKKEN, Anton 57 Christian
57
LIEDLE, Christine 102
LIESE, Wilhelmina 87 89
LINSE, Wilhelmina 87
LITZ, Sophia 35
LOUISI, Wilhelmina 89
LOUSI, Wilhelmina 87
LUTZ, Anna Mueller Schorzman
94 Jacobine 94 Karl 94
Margaretha 57-58
MAAS, Christina 5
MAGSTADT, John H 28 Lea
Magdalena 28
MAIER, 74
MARTIN, Jacobine 94

MEHRER, Christian Sr 109
Gottfried 70 72
METH, Juliana 46
METTLER, ---- 12 Chris 26
Johanna 26 Pauline 12
MILLER, August 54 Pastor 55
Sarah 68
MIND, 69
MINDT, 69
MITCHELL, Mrs 9
MITSEL, Magdalena 46
MITZEL, Magdalena 46
MORGAN, F B 43
MUEHLBEIER, Anna Maria Maas
38 Catharine 38 Catharine
(Katherina) 37 Christina 112
Tobias M 38
MUELLER, (Muller) 36 Albert 69
Amalia 35-36 Anna 93 Dorthea
67 Fredericka 8 Friedericka 67
Friederika 66 Friedricka 68
Georg Jr 66 Georg Sr 66
George 68 Gustav(e) 69 Herbert
69 Jacobine 67 Johanna 67
Johanna Guent(h)ner 66 Joseph
36 Karolina 66 Katerina
Dorothea Bub 36 Martha
Louisa 69 Michael Friedrich 67
Norine 53 Paulina Helena 69
Phillip 68 Rebecca 70 Regina
68 Rose 68 Rosina 66 W
Wilhelm 8 66-67 Wilhelm 5-6
51 67-68 117
MUELLER(?), Katherina Diede
Kusler 42
MUEND, 69
MUHLAUSER, Philippine 114
MUHLEISEN, Anna Maria 48 77
MULBEYER, (Muehlbeier) David
57 (Muehlbeier) Katharina 57
MULLER, Amelia 36 Anna
Margareta 48 Anna Maria 48 77
Catharina 36 49 59

MULLER (cont.)
Catharina Barbara 48 Catherine
46 Christian 48 77 Jacobine 36
Jakob 48 77 Josef 36 Julie 36
Lydia 36 Paul 36 Rebekka 48
76-77 Regina 48 Wilhelm 103
Wm 68
MUND, Adam 69 Catherina 69
Elizabeth 69 Georg 69 George 69
Heinrich 69 Jacob 69 Katie 69
MUNSCH, Christina 19 Elizabeth
58 64 Elizabetha 62
MUTSCHELKNAUS, (Jakobine)
Barbara (Heinle) 77 Barbara 77
Bertha 75 Caroline 70 Christina
77 Ema 75 Emil 75 Friedrich 60
70 74-77 Gottlieb 51 75 77
Gustoph 75 Jacob 48 75 Jacob
Jr 41 Jakob 70 72-73 75-77
Johann 75 Julius 75 Karl 75
Karolina 75 Maria 77 Rebecca
75 Rebecca Mueller 70
Rebekka 48 76-77 Regina 75
Wilhelmine 77
NEUBAUER, F 42
NEUHARTH, Christian 95
Christine 95 Johanna 95
ORTH, Bertha 28 Elizabeth 64
Margaret Nee Schmidt 28
Martha 28 William 28 64
PETERSON, Albert 8 Elizabeth 8
PFAFF, Fred 42 Magdalena 103-
104
PFUESTER, Maria 116
PRESZLER, John 92 Philip 65
Regina 65 92
PUDWILL, Henry 26 Paulina 26
RADAK, Emanuel 35 Rosina 35
RADKE, Salomine 12
RATH, George 83 111
RATHKE, Rebecca 35
REDINGER, Michael 19
Wilhelmina 19

SCHAMBER (cont.)
 Johannes Georg 89 John 86-88
 Ludwig 86-87 Margaret 87 89
 Maria 88 Martin 66 87 89 Otto
 88 Pauline 91 94 Peter 68 89
 Peter (1) 87 89 Peter (2) 89-92
 Regina 92 Robert 88 Rosina 87
 89 Rosine 89 Sophie 87 Susan
 89 92 Susana 90-91 Udo 88
 Wilhelmina 87 89-90 92
 Willma 90
SCHATZ, Anna Maria 3 85
 Barbara 2 Christina Herzel 2
 Jacob 2 Katharina 102 Regina
 68
SCHEMP, Elizabeth 64
SCHEMPP, Emma 36 Gottlieb 6
 Magdalena 85
SCHEPT, Georg 37 Karl 37
 Katharina 37
SCHIERMEISTER, Carolina 121
SCHINDLER, Johanna 45 Rosina
 55
SCHMELZEL, Theresa 35
SCHMIDTGALL, Jacobina 12
SCHMOLL, Magdalena 65
SCHNAIDT, Jacob 88
SCHOECK, Elisabeth 115
 Elisabetha 116 Ernst 116 Georg
 Heinrich 115 Maria 116
SCHOOK, M 56
SCHOPPERT, John 55 Pauline 55
SCHORTZMAN, 92 Christian 93
 Johann 93 Magdalena 93 Maria
 Margaretha 93 Rosina 93
SCHORZMAN, Andrew 95 Anna
 Mueller 93-95 August 92 94
 Barbara 93 Bertha 92 Carolina
 93 Catharina 93 Catherine 94
 Christ 94 Christian 94
 Christiana 95 Christina 94
 Christine 93-95 David 95
 Emelia 94-95 Gottlieb 94

SCHORZMAN (cont.)
 Heinrich 92-93 Jacob 94 Johann
 92-95 Johann Adam 93-94
 Johann Adam Sr 92 Johann
 Jacob 93 Johanna 95 Johannes
 93 Johannestal 93 John 94
 Julius 95 Katherine 94 Louise
 94-95 Margaret 94-95
 Margareta 93 Margareth 93
 Margret 95 Mathilda 93 Meta
 95 Pauline 94 Theodore 95
SCHORZMANN, 92
SCHOTZMANN, 92
SCHRAMM, Christina 95 Eduard
 95 Emma 96 Ferdinand P 95
 George Mueller 96 Heinrich 95
 Herbert 95 Ida Theresa 95
 Jacob 95-96 Jacobina 95 Jakob
 95 Johann 95-96 Margareth 95
 Pauline 95 Phillipina 95
SCHRINK, Louisa 65
SCHULZ, Anna Dorothea 120
 Daniel 120 Johann 120
 Wilhelmina 120
SCHUMK, ---- 12 Lydia Maria
 Magdalena 12
SERR, Catherina Engel 122
 Christian 96 Christina 45 96
 Christine 102 Christoph 96
 Edward 103 Fredericka 103
 Georg 96 Henry 123 Henry M
 102 Jacob 96 Jacob M 102
 Joanna 103 Johann 96 Johann
 Christoph 96 Johanna (Hanna)
 Kost 96 John 123 John Michael
 103 Karolina 103 Katharina 96-
 97 Katharina Engel 67 102
 Katharina Schatz 102 Katherina
 8 103 Michael 8 11 67 96-97
 102-103 122 Pauline 103
 Regina 64 Robert Emil 103
 Rosina 97 103
SEYDEL, Margareth 93 Peter 93

WALSH, J 10
WALZ, Martha Louisa 69
WEBER, Agnesia Bauer 29
    Carolina 114 Christina 4
    Doretha 114 Elisabetha 1 Elma
    4 Johannes 29 Konrad 114
    Richard 4
WEIDENBACH, (Georg) Heinrich
    Sr 118 Amelia 14 114 117-118
    Anna Margaretta 46 115 Cath
    116 Catharina 117 Catherine
    115 Christina 117 Elisa 116
    Elisabeth 39 115 117-118
    Elizabeth 46 51 54 115 117
    Eugene 116 Eva Katharina 115
    Eva Katharina Michel 114
    Frederich 117 Friederika 117
    Friederika Jungmann 115 118
    Friedricke 116 Georg Heinrich
    46 George Heinrich 115 Heh
    116 Hein 116 Heinrich 33 114-
    115 117 Heinrich Jr 81 116 118
    Heinrich Sr 115-116 Johann
    Konrad 114 Kasper 115 Konrad
    115 117 Lydia 118 Margareth
    115 Maria Katharina 115 Marie
    116 Philippine 114 Richard 19
    Rosina 19 Sibylla 115 Wilh 116
    Wilhelm 117 Wilhelmina 118
WEIDNER, Susan 89 Susana 90 92
WEIKUM, Katharina 45
WELFEA, Christine 64
WENDSCHLAAG, Henrietha 6
WERNER, Anton 119 Barbara
    Stauss 119 Christina 119 David
    119 Friederick 119 Jakob 119
    Johanna (Ana) 119 Johannes
    119 Katharina 119 Margaretha
    119

WERNER (cont.)
    Maria Elisabeth 119 Phillipina
    119 Wilhelm 119
WIND (MIND?), George 111
WINKEL, Minnie 53
WINTER, Alida R 37 Arthur 37
    121 Daniel 120 Dorethea
    (Dora) 121 Edward 121
    Henride (Henriette) 120 Louisa
    120 Marie Jarcho 120 Mathilda
    120 Matilda 121 Rebecka 120
    Robert 120 Rudolph 121 Simon
    120-121 Sophia Auch Horst 3
    Wilhelmina 120-121 William
    121
WISSER, Rosa 123
WRIGHT, Emilie 40 Harry 40
WUEST, Johanna 32
ZEEB, Elisabeth 117 Peter 67 117
ZEEBACH, J E 43
ZIEGELE, Alexander 122 Carl
    121-122 Carl M 8 Carolina 121
    Edward 122 Elisabetha 121-122
    Elisabetha Brenneisen 121
    Emanuel 122 Emil 122
    Frederick 122 Friederika 121
    Gottlieb 121 Johann 121 Johann
    Jr 122 Johann Sr 122 Johanna
    123 Julia 123 Karl 11 Karolina
    123 Katharina Barbara 121
    Magdalena 121 Margaretha 121
    Marie 8 122 Michael 121 Peter
    122 Philipp 121 Rosina 121-
    123 Saroara 122 Sophia 121-
    122 Wilhelm 122
ZIEGLE, Carl 123
ZIMMERMAN, Anna Maria 81
    Regina 48 Stephan 48

Made in the USA
Las Vegas, NV
14 August 2021

28135563R00092